FIRST WORDS

FIRST WORDS

A Parent's Step-by-Step Guide to Helping a Child with Speech and Language Delays

Barbara Levine Offenbacher

ROWMAN & LITTLEFIELD PUBLISHERS, INC.

Lanham • Boulder • New York • Toronto • Plymouth, UK

All illustrations by Kinga Domitrz

Published by Rowman & Littlefield Publishers, Inc.
A wholly owned subsidiary of The Rowman & Littlefield Publishing Group, Inc.
4501 Forbes Boulevard, Suite 200, Lanham, Maryland 20706
www.rowman.com

10 Thornbury Road, Plymouth PL6 7PP, United Kingdom

British Library Cataloguing in Publication Information Available

Library of Congress Cataloging-in-Publication Data
Offenbacher, Barbara Levine, 1953-
    First words : a parent's step-by-step guide to helping a child with speech and language delays / Barbara Levine Offenbacher.
        p. cm.
    ISBN 978-1-4422-1122-3 (cloth : alk. paper)—ISBN 978-1-4422-1124-7 (electronic)
    1. Speech disorders in children. 2. Language disorders in children. I. Title.
RJ496.S7O34 2013
618.92'855—dc23   2012026710

♾™ The paper used in this publication meets the minimum requirements of American National Standard for Information Sciences—Permanence of Paper for Printed Library Materials, ANSI/NISO Z39.48-1992.

Printed in the United States of America

This book is dedicated
to the memory of my devoted and loving parents
Joseph and Jean Levine ז״ל
Who taught me the *art* of communication

&

The Department of Speech and Language
Brooklyn College, City University of New York
Who taught me the *science*

"I am not a man of words...
for I am heavy of mouth and heavy of speech."
Exodus 4:10

לא איש דברים אנכי כי כבד פה וכבד לשון אנכי

CONTENTS

PART FOUR: VERBATIM SAMPLES OF SPECTRUM LANGUAGE DISORDERS

PART FIVE: HOW TO NATURALLY ADVANCE YOUR CHILD'S COMMUNICATION DEVELOPMENT WITHOUT MISSING VALUABLE OPPORTUNITIES

ACKNOWLEDGMENTS

I am forever indebted to the Speech Department at Brooklyn College, CUNY. During my undergraduate and graduate years, I had the opportunity to learn with the best and the brightest in the field. As a college freshman, it was Margaret Flynn, who inspired me to pursue this most amazing career. I had the distinct privilege of knowing and being trained by Drs. Oliver Bloodstein, Roberta Chapey, John Duffy, Gail Gurland, Irving Hochberg, and Harriet Klein, all trailblazers. In addition to the speech pathology and audiology program, I was also trained in education of the speech and hearing handicapped. I thank Esther Bogin and Beryl Adler for their wonderful teaching, and guidance. They were my instructors at the college, as well as my mentors, during my student teaching experience, in the New York City public school system. Straight out of grad school I landed my first job at PS 255, a public school in Brooklyn, New York, which housed both a mainstream and special education program. I remained in that position for eight years, under the remarkable supervision of Susan Lee Rein, the perfect Burberry/Brooks Brothers sophisticate. There is no doubt that my success as a clinician goes to Susan. Her hours of observations, her scrutiny over every detail of my therapy plans, her endless suggestions on how to make therapy more creative and effective, and her allegiance to the unprecedented, special education laws, newly passed by the U.S. Supreme Court, made her the unquestionable master clinician. Susan demanded accountability and parental involvement in therapy. Her influence and guidance, remains unyielding to this day. In addition to all this, I was extremely fortunate to be trained during a very exciting time.

The 1980s was a revolutionary period in special education, and a revolutionary time in speech and language research. New names dominated the field, Lois Bloom and Margaret Lahey, Elizabeth Wigg and Eleanor Semel with their work in language development; and Barbara Hodson and Harriet Klein with their work in phonological processing. These women reinvented the profession; they were the new pioneers. I studied from their textbooks and research. I attended workshops, seminars, and conventions where I had the opportunity to further my education and training through their groundbreaking contributions to the field. I am equally grateful to them for their outstanding impact, and how their work has made me a better clinician. Now, with the current revolution in the study of cognitive sciences, artificial intelligence, and the brain; the work of Noam Chomsky, Eric Kandel, and Steven Pinker are introducing me to the newest frontier. Their work too, continues to make me a better clinician. I am grateful to all these professionals, my timing could not have been better.

Currently, I am engaged in a full time private practice. The parents I have met and the children I have worked with have made a permanent impact on my life. Over the years I have acquired priceless friendships, and an immeasurable amount of support. I am grateful to all those parents who entrusted me with their children; I want them to know that I worked tirelessly to make a positive and lasting impact. I am also gratified by the many teachers, and school administrators who spent numerous hours via phone, meetings, and emails collaborating, in order to bridge effective therapy, with the classroom curriculum. Successful therapy requires two essential ingredients; a partnership between clinician, parent, school, and accountability. I am indebted to all those who gave so much of their time.

Writing this book is a project that began over twenty years ago. As my career moved forward, it became apparent that the time I spent in therapy with any individual child was just not enough. There were too many waking hours in the day, at risk, of being unproductive. Since every experience is an opportunity for language growth, whether walking down the aisle of a supermarket, or fishing, I knew that I needed to embrace the active participation of parents to fill this potential void. In addition, it also became apparent that valuable time was being lost as parents waited past their child's second birthday to hear a first word, and still waited, not knowing the importance of early testing and intervention. Nor did they have strategies to help stimulate their child's speech and language development, as they waited for therapy to begin. Parents needed to become empowered, and that's what this book is all about. I want to thank the publishers at Rowman and Littlefield for accepting my manuscript, and recognizing the need for this book. I also want to thank Patti Davis for her input during the early stages of the publishing process, and to Jin Yu and Laura Grzybowski for their input during the final stages. It has been a pleasure working with these most professional women. I also want to thank my book agent, Sheree Bykofsky, and her colleague Janet Rosen. Together they have answered my questions, given me sound advice, and guided me through this process. A special thanks to Sheree for all her work concerning the negotiation of the final contract. I can't imagine a better book agent exists than Sheree.

Over the years I have been blessed by wonderful colleagues. I want to thank Shaindy Guttman Cohen for the years we spent together; as well as the many undergraduate and graduate students whom I mentored. I also want to thank my friend and colleague, JoAnn Sokoloff. She taught me everything I know about creativity, and grant writing. Special thanks go to Rachelle and Ben-Gurion Matsas, founders of Image Magazine, and their sons, Steven and Michael. They have given me the opportunity to write dozens of articles, enabling me to inform countless families on issues regarding child speech and language development. Their magazine has had a significant impact on the success of my practice, and as a result, I will be forever appreciative. In addition, I am thankful to the Audiology Department at Long Island College Hospital. Over the years I have referred many children for Central Auditory Processing Testing. Their expertise has played a key role in helping to identify the presence of language learning disabilities, thus enabling appropriate diagnosis and treatment. I also want to thank Drs. Roberta Chapey PhD, and Harriet Klein PhD, noted professors in the field of speech and language; as well as Drs. Cece McCarton MD, and Eddie Gindi MD, both board certified pediatricians, in developmental and general pediatrics respectively, for taking their valuable time to review the book. I am personally honored by their support. Words cannot begin to express my genuine gratitude to Kay Domitrz. Kay and I have been a team for over ten years. It's hard to believe that when we first met Kay was searching for a career. Now, after receiving her BA and masters degree in speech and language pathology from Brooklyn College; Kay, a clinician in the New York City public school system, is working toward her bilingual certification at Columbia University. I collaborated with Kay countless times during the many drafts of this book, and could not have completed it without her. Thankfully, she has left an indelible mark by drawing the various illustrations. I have no doubt that Kay will have an amazing future. Lastly, my sincere thanks go to Dr. Michael DeMeo. "My success is your success."

Finally, over the many years of my career, my family has witnessed the countless hours I have dedicated to this endeavor. I am truly thankful for their patience and tolerance. I want to thank my husband Dr. Eliezer Offenbacher, who has recognized the labor of this book, as an important personal and professional goal. I know he takes pride in my career success, and is proud that I have accomplished this endeavor. To my daughter in law, Rachel, you are a gift. You have given my life new meaning in more ways than you can possibly imagine, not to mention making me a grandma. I love you Ari! To my sons, Joseph and Richard, there is nothing in life that can compare to my unconditional love, and devotion to you both. You have grown up to be the kind of young adults parents dream of. I am so proud to be your mother. In closing, I thank G-d for bringing me to this place in my life.

Barbara Levine Offenbacher, 2012

Part One

TYPICAL SPEECH AND LANGUAGE DEVELOPMENT AND DISORDER

INTRODUCTION

Why Are You Reading This Book?

You are reading this book because you are concerned about your child's speech and language development. You want to learn more about why her communication is delayed, and what you can do to help. Although you do not want to overreact, the possibility of autism spectrum disorder (ASD) is on your mind. I want you to understand that this book is not intended to be a substitute for a qualified licensed speech and language clinician. No book could assume that role. However, a book can be informative, instructional, and helpful.

More than sixty years ago, Dr. Benjamin Spock led the way in self-help reading with his famous book, *Baby and Child Care*. It energized the creation of the twentieth-century proactive parent. Mothers and fathers had a source to explain typical children's maladies and health issues. It eased the layperson's fears with practical advice and useful information. The book earned importance as a symbol of parents' desire to help and comfort their children.

THE BOOK'S GOAL

That is the goal of this book, to give you direction in order to help your speech and language delayed child. It provides valuable insight into typical speech and language development, and ways for you to help stimulate your child's communication. In my clinical experience, children delayed in speech and language are often not identified until 2-3 years old, with therapy beginning between 2.5–3 years. If you consider that between 2.5–4 years old, typically developing children can say most speech sounds, use 200 to 300 words and speak in two- and three-word sentences, your child can fall behind very quickly. When it comes to language delay, or concern about ASD, the literature points to the belief that the earlier the intervention, the better the outcome. In other words, time is a critical factor.

There are many books on the subject of ASD, so why should you choose this book? What makes this book different? Currently, many books on ASD fall into two categories, anecdotal and informative. The anecdotal books, often written by mothers, tell their personal story. They are a chronicle of events, beginning with the first signs of their child's withdrawal, the diagnosis of pervasive developmental delay (PDD), or ASD, followed by hard work and dedication. The second category I refer to as informative. These books are resources for getting help. They focus on medical and family issues, legal rights, and special education.

This book is different because it focuses only on speech and language development, and how you can assume the role of a speech partner to help stimulate your child's communication development. Your goal is to awaken your child's ability and desire to communicate. You want her to discover that communication is a way to fulfill her needs and wants. This guide will give you constructive ideas and strategies to use with her. I will tell you the types of toys to have and how to play with them. I will show you how to set up a play-learning area in your home and how it should be designed. I will also provide you with more than 700 vocabulary words your child should know, along with checklists to record your child's performance. As your child advances I will show you how to develop the use of two words, short phrases, and simple sentences. I also created what I will refer to as language experience plans. These plans will have word lists and word phrases appropriate for everyday experiences, such as baking cookies and doing laundry. You will be able to include your child in these visual, hands-on experiences while focusing on developing language at the same time. As a seasoned therapist I know there is a lot that you can do and a lot you can learn. I am dedicated to sharing my knowledge and years of experience with you.

BECOMING PROACTIVE

Even if your child has already been evaluated, the process from testing to therapy may take weeks if not months. In fact, even when therapy does begin, there are many hours of the day, weekends, and holidays when you will be without the guidance and assistance of your therapist. I don't want you to wait while valuable time is slipping by. With me, the therapist by your side, we will begin the journey together, to find your child's hidden voice.

Lastly, before we get started, and I cannot stress this last point enough... If you have any, and I stress again, *any* concern regarding your child's hearing discuss this with your pediatrician immediately. Be sure to have your child's hearing tested. Deafness, hearing loss, or chronic middle ear infections may be the reason why your child is delayed in speech and language development.

You are now ready to embark on a fact-finding mission to help your language delayed child. I sincerely hope that this book helps you help your child.

❶

MY CHILD IS NOT SPEAKING

As parents we anxiously watch our children grow, waiting for each developmental milestone to emerge. Every month from birth there are new expectations. When will my child sit, crawl, walk? Although every milestone is important, speech and language development is unique. We wait for our child's first words with an unparalleled excitement. Finally, the mystery behind their cries can be expressed. In this chapter, I am going to explain the ramifications of when a child is not speaking.

There is a critical window of opportunity, between eighteen and twenty-four months, when children are expected to typically develop speech and language skills. There is no question that children develop differently. Some say words at fourteen months, others at twenty-four months. My concern is when your child has bypassed the expected window of time.

There is reason for anxiety. According to the Centers for Disease Control and Prevention, autism spectrum disorder (ASD) occurs in 1 in 88 births in the United States, and is the fastest growing developmental disability, with a 10–17 percent annual growth rate. With early diagnosis and intervention, the cost of lifelong care can be reduced by two-thirds.

DIAGNOSIS

Prior to five years old, professionals are reluctant to label a child with a definitive diagnosis. This is because a child may go through maturational changes, and what appeared to be a developmental delay turns out to be something different. In order to generically identify a significant delay in the acquisition of speech and language, the term PDD, pervasive/pediatric developmental delay, is widely used for children between the ages of three and five. In addition, it is often difficult to make a diagnosis before five years of age since different characteristics of a variety of language learning disorders may overlap, such as central auditory processing disorder (CAPD), or executive function disorder. As a result, the diagnosis of autism is typically not given until five years old. By five, the diagnosis is made based upon the identification of characteristics typical of the disorder. Currently, we are learning more about autism through brain imaging research; however, the diagnosis continues to be made by observation.

Although children develop differently, there is a window of time when different milestones are expected to emerge. For decades, many mothers have been accused of being neurotic, when they would express their worries regarding their child's developmental delays. This is no longer the case. We have justifiable reason, from evidence-based research, to be concerned. If you believe that your child's speech and language development is delayed, do not wait. Contact your child's pediatrician and arrange for an evaluation.

FUSSY BABIES

The Beginning Signs

In this chapter I am going to discuss behaviors of fussy babies. Sometimes fussy behaviors continue through the toddler and early childhood years. These behaviors may be the beginning sign of ASD. On the other hand they may be nothing more than a passing phase. There are other situations where poor parenting skills create maladaptive behaviors. These behaviors have the potential to be confused with a developmental disorder. The following short scenarios will illustrate.

FIVE STORIES

Story #1: Many babies are fussy and sensitive. Some continuously cry, cannot be put down, and cannot easily be consoled. No matter what you do, you just can't seem to comfort your baby. Babies have many adjustments to make. They need to cope with hunger, wet diapers, discomfort, even an itchy tag on their undershirt, helplessly unable to communicate any of their distresses. This is enough to put an adult into red alert. In most situations your baby is fine. This fussy time will pass, leaving very tired, worn-out parents who cannot remember when they had their last full night of sleep!

Story #2: Another challenging time is typical during the toddler years. Although your child will be more capable of communicating his needs and wants, temper tantrums and other defiant issues surrounding bedtime, food choices, and dressing may bring you to the point of exasperation. Be brave! By sending clear messages to your child, establishing age-appropriate rules, and consistently reinforcing them, your child will learn how to meet her needs and wants in socially appropriate ways. You'll join the ranks of many parents who retell classic stories at every birthday party, "Remember when Jake wrote across the carpet with my red lipstick?" Many parents have a collection of these events.

Story #3: From the time your child was born you felt something was wrong. He was always hypersensitive to light, sound, and touch. He never enjoyed being held, and seemed to stiffen his body when he was in your arms. Neither a bottle, a toy, nor a ride in the carriage could distract him from crying. By his second birthday he seemed to be in his own world. He was not speaking, making eye contact, or playing appropriately. Your pediatrician is concerned, but takes a wait-and-see attitude.

Story #4: On the other hand, you may have watched your baby developing typically, reaching major milestones within the expected window of time. Then suddenly, there is a change. For no apparent reason your child stops talking, appears withdrawn, and avoids eye contact. Your instincts tell you this change in behavior is alarming. Don't wait. Schedule a speech and language evaluation as soon as possible.

Story #5: I have known children between the ages of three and five rejected from mainstream nursery and kindergarten programs because their behavior was incorrectly diagnosed as a disorder. The reason for this error in interpretation: poor parenting skills. From early on, some parents are micromanagers. Beginning at infancy, the home temperature is adjusted to equal the fetal environment, snowsuits answer the alarm of sudden cool temperatures in November, and coverings over baby's head and face defend against wind. Worst is when this mobile shelter remains in place inside the supermarket! During the toddler and early childhood years some parents are poor managers. They attend to every cry and wish of their three-year-old at minuteman speed. When asked, "Why do you do this?" the answer is typically the same. "I want my child to know how much I love him," or, "I only want her to be happy." Children learn, "If I cry or throw a tantrum long enough, I'll get the candy," and they do! They learn maladaptive ways to manipulate their parents and control their world.

By preschool, the child is incapable of following directions, sharing, cooperating, or waiting her turn. She doesn't understand appropriate social boundaries, she has difficulty attending to a task, and lacks impulse control. All this begins to interfere with learning. By four years old she has a reputation, and it's not a good one. Disguised as love, parents can innocently create a maladapted child.

Parenting skills have a tremendous impact on childhood development. At a young age, a fine line exists between behaviors that are developmentally disordered, and behaviors that are environmentally disordered. Misguided parenting can innocently create the appearance of a hyperactivity disorder, oppositional behavior disorder, or executive function disorder.

Through these examples, you have seen many different ways children develop and adapt to their environment. Some behaviors they are born with, others they learn. Similar childhood behaviors overlap. Are these behaviors a warning sign of a disorder, a passing phase, or the result of misguided parenting? As you can see during the early childhood years, a very fine line exists between a real disorder and a learned disorder. It is important to be aware of your child's behaviors, as well as your own. Remember, parenting is powerful and directly impacts on your child's development. Don't create unnecessary problems. If you have any doubts about your child's development, trust your instincts and speak with your child's pediatrician. If you feel you need help with parenting, speak with a psychologist.

TRUST YOUR INSTINCTS

It is hard to judge if your baby's fussy behavior is indicative of a problem. It is not until you start to look back over months, maybe even a year, that you notice those finicky behaviors were really warning signals. You realize that when you look at old photos or home videos, taken between your child's first and second birthdays, the explosive episodes in the park, disinterest in the funny clown, and the obsession with the wheel on the wagon were all symptoms of an underlying, significant, developmental delay. What happens when your child is not adapting to the environment, when everyday occurrences are presenting too much anxiety, when his tolerance level is overloaded like a fuse, and cannot be readily calmed or consoled? He's not looking at you, and he's acting as if he is deaf. And the bigger question, what happens when he does not appear to be outgrowing this stage? If anything, it appears to be getting worse.

SIGNS OF AUTISM: THE CHECKLIST

Have you noticed your toddler rocking, engaging in repetitive finger play, playing with a single toy the same way over and over without signs of boredom; or aloof to what's going on around him, disconnected, continuously engaged in monotonous activity unless you stop it, excessively reacting with tantrums when it comes to change, inconsolable or difficult to calm, does not appear to know you?

These are the most profound signs that point to a diagnosis of autism, but they are not the only signs. Some children have more subtle characteristics. Autism is referred to as a spectrum disorder. A spectrum is defined as a range or array of characteristics. Autism spectrum disorder presents a range of functioning from low to high. Low functioning children with autism are usually nonverbal, may demonstrate self-destructive behavior, and do not relate to others. Their socialization skills are seriously impaired. Children on the higher end of the autistic spectrum are diagnosed with Asperger syndrome. These children may be of average or better intelligence. Although higher functioning and more socially capable, socialization skills remain a lifelong challenge. The classic difference between autism and Asperger syndrome is that children with Asperger develop speech and language skills within the expected time frame. Those diagnosed with autism may develop speech and language late, if at all.

In this chapter we have learned that from infancy through the early childhood years maladaptive behavior may be the result of a developmental disorder, a passing phase, or a learned response. By eighteen months, if your child is delayed in speech and language onset, resists making eye contact, is socially withdrawn, and ignores your efforts to get his attention, your child may be at risk for ASD. It is most important that you discuss this with your child's pediatrician, and consult a speech and language clinician as soon as possible. Taking a wait-and-see approach may waste valuable time. It will be better in the long run to face your anxieties and move forward. Early intervention is key.

3

THE DEVELOPMENTAL PROCESS

In the previous chapter I discussed the most obvious signs of a child at risk for ASD. However, time may prove that what was originally thought to be ASD was really delayed speech and language development. With that possibility in mind, it is important for you to understand the typical developmental course of communication, and continue to make every effort to stimulate your child accordingly. The process begins by making sounds, developing sustained eye contact, responding with smiles, and recognizing different voices, all of which are the building blocks of social connections. In this chapter you will learn how babies make discoveries about early communication.

SOUNDS

Making sound begins at birth with your baby's first cry. During the first year, your baby will experiment with sounds. This phase is known as babbling. We are entertained by the cooing and gooing sounds babies make. We watch them smiling, kicking, and waving as they feel, hear, and discover new sounds. We babble in response as we play with our babies. It is a constant concert of consonant and vowel sounds. We make eye contact and begin to establish physical and emotional connections. Besides stimulating sound communication we are also inspiring social development.

SOCIALIZATION AND MAKING SOUNDS

Can your child make eye contact?
Can your child sustain eye contact for more than five seconds?
Does your child appear happy?
Does your child smile and laugh when making sounds?
Does your child appear to be interacting with you?
Does your child make different sounds?

If you answer no to two or more of these questions have your child evaluated by a speech and language clinician.

SOCIALIZATION AND THE VOICE

Our voice is also a source of communication. It adds music, loudness, and emotion to a message. Whether you are singing, reading, or speaking to your baby, the expression of your voice varies by changes in rhythm, beat, and loudness. Your baby will respond to the musical tones of your voice as it rises and falls, conveying different feelings. Babies will also respond to how the loudness of your voice changes from a calming lullaby, whisper, or shout.

Is your child overly sensitive to sound?
Does your child cry when there are changes in noise?
Does your child ignore sounds and seem disinterested?
Does your child act as if he is deaf?

If you answer yes to one or more of these questions have your child evaluated.

Does your child turn his head toward the direction of sounds, especially
  if they are sudden or loud?
If you call to your child, will he turn toward your direction?
Does your child seem to recognize your voice?
Does your child enjoy listening?

If you answer no to one or more of these questions have your child evaluated.

EARLY SOUNDS, EARLY COMMUNICATION

Different cries are the earliest signs of communication. Infants are able to communicate feelings of comfort and discomfort by their cries. As time goes on, your baby's sounds will be linked with experiences. Your baby will make sounds related to comfort or pain. These are the first sounds of communication. Babies do not learn these sounds. They discover them.

HOW DO BABIES DISCOVER SOUNDS?

As babies move, they make sounds. As babies respond to the functions of their own bodies, they make sounds. What is more amazing is that during this period infants are all making the same discoveries. It is universal. This is what infants do! Infants have been shown to have different desires to vocalize. For example, an infant may make sounds in the bath that are different than those sounds made in the crib. They also make different sounds when they are with different people, or when they are engaged with a familiar object such as a soft toy, mobile, or bottle. When these objects are taken away, infants make different sounds as well. This early sensitivity is the beginning of the relationship between sound and meaning. Discovering and experimenting with sound is a pleasurable, developmental experience for babies. It is so pleasurable and natural that they keep doing it over and over again.

As you can see, communication begins early in a baby's life. The combination of sound, voice, facial expression, and eye contact all work in tandem to stimulate the development of speech, language, and socialization. It's universal. Babies do the same thing at the same time all over the world. Within the first few months of life these elements of communication develop rapidly. As children approach their first birthday they begin to zone in on the language their parents speak. Language concepts advance, culminating in your child's first words, typically between twelve and eighteen months of age. In the next chapter I am going to explain the difference between speech, language, and mother tongue. These are important terms relevant to understanding communication development. Knowing these terms will enable you to better understand your own child's development, and empower you to be an effective advocate if your child should require speech and language services.

SPEECH, LANGUAGE, AND MOTHER TONGUE

The Communication Process

You just read about the earliest components of communication: sound, voice, facial expression, and eye contact. Now you are going to read about the essence of communication, the interpersonal achievement of speech and language. It's the platinum membership card uniquely held by the human race. But what exactly are speech, language, and mother tongue? Are they the same process, or are they different? Does language mean English or Spanish? Do we need to learn this task or is it automatic?

WHAT IS SPEECH?

Think of speech as a tool of human communication. It is the way we send and receive messages. Speech is not the only way to convey a message. Dance, music, Morse code, and hand signs are also ways to communicate. To get a better understanding, let's look at Morse code. Dots and dashes are used to send messages. Think of these dots and dashes as speech sounds. They are the way the message is transmitted. Random, individual dots and dashes do not have meaning. The dots and dashes need to be arranged in a way that spells out a meaningful message, such as ...---... (the code for SOS). Any other arrangement of these dots and dashes would change the meaning.

Most people communicate using speech. Speech is the most common tool we use to send a message. Just like in Morse code, speech sounds cannot be random. They have to be organized in a purposeful way to produce meaningful words. If we agree that speech is a tool, a way to communicate, then language is the meaning.

WHAT IS LANGUAGE?

One of the earliest recorded documents on language and meaning comes from the Old Testament, found in the Book of Genesis.

It was the time of Babel:

> The whole earth was of one language and of common purpose. Instead of being satisfied the people caused a great upheaval and rebelled. They were punished, and their words were confused so they should not understand one another's language and from there G-d scattered them over the face of the whole earth.

Without a unifying language system, chaos ensues. Just like what happened in Babel. You cannot establish a society, build a nation, or fashion a community without understanding one another. Language is a system of ideas that is understood for the purpose of communication. It is made up of sounds, ideas, words, sentences, and grammar rules. However, just knowing this is not enough; there needs to be meaning.

WHAT IS MOTHER TONGUE?

The language we learn to speak from our parents is called our mother tongue. My mother tongue is English!

For speech and language to be meaningful, sounds need to be combined into words that we understand. Then through experience and knowledge about the world we develop ideas. Words need to be arranged in a specific order, following the rules of your mother tongue. Sentences need to be set in sequence, especially in writing, and rules of grammar need to be followed to show understanding of ideas.

HOW DO CHILDREN LEARN THIS COMPLEX TASK?

Children begin this task at birth. It is a complex system that develops quickly, where children learn to understand the world around them, build knowledge, and apply the rules of grammar without any formal lessons. By the time children turn five years old, they know how to construct a sentence. Their mastery of language and grammatical understanding is like an adult's; they are fully equipped. The difference is that children talk about different things than grown-ups. Here is an example:

Jonathan, thirty-five years old: "I found a great house. I'm applying for a mortgage."

Jennifer, five years old: "I saw a Dora lunchbox. I want one for school."

Different topics . . . grammatically equivalent.

HOW DO CHILDREN DO THIS?

The human brain comes preprogrammed, equipped with an instinct to develop language. Steven Pinker, a contemporary cognitive neuroscientist, has conducted extensive research in child language acquisition; he describes language development as follows:

> Language is not a cultural artifact that we learn the way we learn to tell time or how the federal government works. Instead, it is a distinct piece of the biological makeup of our brains. Language is a complex, specialized skill, which develops in the child spontaneously, without conscious effort or formal instruction, is deployed without awareness of its underlying logic, (and) is qualitatively the same in every individual. (*The Language Instinct*)

In other words, language is an "instinct." To highlight the point, Pinker makes this powerful comparison: "People know how to talk . . . [like] spiders know how to spin webs."

We just know how to do it! We are born with an ability to learn a language system in any of the four thousand languages known to exist. Children learn to speak at the same time, in the same way, and even start saying the same words all around the world. Universal grammar explains this phenomenon.

WHAT IS UNIVERSAL GRAMMAR?

Universal grammar is a strategy that children are born with. It works for the grammatical development of all languages. Around six months of age babies begin to babble or play with sounds. Interestingly, babbling sounds are the same for all children in all languages. Around ten months of age, babies begin to make a language shift. They start to zone in on the speech sounds their parents use.

Here is an example of a language shift. A child in Sweden is born with the same ability to learn the rules of language as a child born in the United States. The child in Sweden will listen, start to distinguish sounds, and learn the rules of Swedish. The child in the United States will listen, distinguish sounds, and learn the rules of English.

When children are exposed to the speech of their parents' language, they begin to specify the language they will eventually learn. This is the language of your mother tongue. In other words, children all around the world start off with the same program to learn language. They have a universal potential. Sound specialization and sound sorting ultimately results in one child learning to speak English, another Spanish, Hebrew, and so on for the four thousand languages around the world.

Like a tree, speech, language, and mother tongue are branches growing from a single trunk. Instinctively, the tree knows how to produce food and grow. The roots take in water that sustains the tree, just like children take in information about the world. They begin with sounds, form words, and develop ideas, a process that will continue throughout their lifetime. Think about all the different trees on earth: apple trees, maple trees, and pine trees, just to name a few. These different trees represent all the different languages spoken around the world. Think of these beautiful, fragrant, sometimes blossoming orchards as an orchestra of human communication. How do these orchards grow? Seeds, sunshine, water, and the air they breathe are the ingredients they need to thrive. How do children begin the process of communication—speech, language, and mother tongue? The answer: experience.

5

LANGUAGE DEVELOPMENT THROUGH EXPERIENCE

In the last chapter we spoke about language as an instinct. When many of us think of the term *instinct*, we imagine the animal kingdom. How amazing it is to see nature able to achieve such a beautiful balance. Seeing animals caring for their young, building homes, and attacking prey appears to be nothing short of a miracle. If acquiring language is a human instinct, does it miraculously develop? How do children know that a flower is called a flower, or a ball that rolls out of sight still exists? In this chapter I will talk about the essential role of communication and experience.

While interacting in their environment, children develop language through experience. Through play they are engaged in visual, hands-on experiences. Children listen as parents talk about what they are doing. Parents talk while their child eats, takes a bath, plays, and dresses. Without even realizing it, parents repeat, stress, and isolate important words. Your language delayed child, especially if he is at risk for ASD, needs these experiences. So you are going to do what your child is not able to do on his own. You are going to systematically pair experiences with words. You are going to work hard to help him break the autism barrier and make his world meaningful.

FOUR STEPS TO STIMULATE LANGUAGE: REPEATING, STRESSING, ISOLATING, QUESTIONING

Repeating

Repeating is an important technique. Your child will need to hear a word used many times in order to associate it with the person, object, or action it represents. Additionally, repetition is the way words and ideas get stored in your child's memory, available to be recalled at another time. Here is an example:

Jake is two and a half years old. He likes to play with cars but there is a problem. He plays with the same car and spins the same wheel all the time. He does not know his toy is called a car, and he does not know what a car does. Let's target the words *car* and *go*. You start by playing with the car. Make sure your child is making eye contact and watching. Show your child the car and say:

"Jake, **car!**" [make sure your child is looking at the car when you say car]
"car"
"car"
"**car** go" [make the car go whenever you say go]
"car go"
"car"
"go"
"go go"
"go car go"
"car"

Repeat, take a break, try again. You will do this multiple times a day over many days until your child can say or sign the words *car* and *go* appropriately. If you feel that your child is not ready for two words, begin with car. Later in the book you will find over seven hundred single words. You will present those words using the same technique as I just described. At the beginning, repetition is critical.

When you are ready to advance to two words, pair car with the following action/verb words:

stop car
park car
wash car
push car
drive car
turn car

Advance to two words pairing car with descriptive/adjective words:

big car
red car
little car
fast car

Stressing

Stressing is when you focus on a particular word. You would say the word louder, slower, and with more stress. So in the repetition example you may want to say the word *car* with more emphasis, or stress the action words *go, stop, park, wash,* or *push*.

Isolating

Isolating is when you separate a word you want to emphasize. This technique is used when you're using short phrases or sentences and you want to bring attention to one of the words.

Questioning

Through questioning you can determine if your child understands what he hears. "What is this?" as you point to the toy car. He needs to be able to understand the question and recall the word *car* from his memory. Here is another example. "Is this a car?" as you point to the toy airplane. Your child needs to be able to identify the plane, and reject the word *car*. This can be a difficult task for a child with ASD. You make the plane go and ask, "What is the plane doing?" He needs to answer flying. The word has to show that he understands how the plane is moving.

Let's review. First, children need to learn words that name people, objects, and actions. Then they need to demonstrate their understanding by answering questions. This may be a slow process. Be patient and follow the four-step model.

HOW DOES THIS HELP LANGUAGE DEVELOPMENT?

This four-step language stimulation activity will help your child process information about the car. This technique should be used for the additional seven hundred words that you will teach your child. Through play she will develop ideas and concepts and increase her knowledge about the world. By answering questions she will demonstrate understanding. Responding to questions will also demonstrate a willingness to communicate and the ability to recall information from his memory. Once your child can appropriately answer questions she will be able to experience meaningful play, talk about objects, and initiate actions. She will now be ready to socialize productively and play with other children.

These small, focused experiences help to develop meaningful language, with the goal of breaking through the autism barrier. By repeating, or narrating while your child is playing, for example with the car, he is able to hear and associate the word with the object, see the object and formulate an image, and learn facts about the object. He will understand what the object is doing, its function, and store the newly acquired information in his memory for later use. Remember, language development for a typically developing child is automatic. For a child delayed or at risk for ASD the language process needs to be learned. Your goal is to introduce your child to meaningful language and guide him through the process.

Experience is the necessary ingredient in stimulating the use of speech and language. There are techniques that help children associate words with people, actions, objects, and events. By repeating, stressing, isolating, and questioning, children learn to assign meaningful words to the world around them. It is a process that takes time. For a child who is language delayed it is more likely that it will take longer. If your child is not using words to communicate by two and a half to three years of age, it should be quite apparent that she is experiencing a significant delay in language. It is imperative that you have your child tested by a speech and language clinician as soon as possible. But in the meantime, what can you do to give your child opportunities to stimulate her language? Where can a parent begin?

6

MY DELAYED THREE-YEAR-OLD

Where Do I Begin?

By now your child should either be in an early intervention program or in the midst of evaluation procedures. Regardless, being proactive means that you want to do everything you can to help your child now. Even if your child is three years of age, if she is not using words, her language age may be between twelve and eighteen months old. To help your child, you need to establish your child's language age. This chapter will give you helpful insight.

Your child is three years old, nonverbal, or repeating words without meaning. For now he does not know the names of objects or their function. He is a passive child, happy to sit playing with his favorite toy. Your neighbor's daughter is also three, and developing typically. She has many words in her vocabulary and speaks in short sentences. You want your child to play with her. Maybe he will catch up if he plays with verbal children.

There is nothing wrong with your three-year-old child playing with her peers. Socialization is important, but if she is nonverbal or confused about the world, her language age may actually be more reflective of a child between twelve and eighteen months old. If she does not know the names of objects and their functions you need to employ the four steps I described in the previous chapter. Remember, even though your child is three, right now her language age is not. The critical factor is that she is challenged by a significant developmental language barrier. Later in this book I will present hundreds of single words, followed by examples of two-word combinations. I will show you how children put words together so you will be able to help your child. I believe a serious mistake is made when language goals are not appropriately and developmentally established. Therefore, in the next chapter I am going to focus on the need and importance of understanding the stages of typical language development.

7

THE STAGES OF LANGUAGE ACQUISITION

There are many stages of language acquisition. If your child is delayed, keep in mind that even though she may be three years old, her language age may be equivalent to eighteen months. Language is a process, and it is important to understand the different stages of typical development. If your child is nonverbal, you will focus on the expectations of that phase; if your child uses single words, you will focus on that stage. This chapter will give you helpful insight.

EARLY LANGUAGE ACQUISITION

Language acquisition is a developmental process. From birth to six months of age your child does not have any plan or intention to communicate. From six to twelve months of age his desire to communicate slowly begins to emerge. It starts with social communication. Social communication develops between you and your baby through eye contact, laughing, and the desire to be held. Babies react happily to familiar faces, voices, and toys. They enjoy when you play with them, and by the end of their first year, they begin to use sounds and cries that have a purpose. Babies want to communicate. Their cries signal, "pick me up, I'm hungry, my diaper is wet, I'm alone in my crib, come get me!"

From twelve to twenty-four months and forward, communication is intentional. The biggest breakthrough is the beginning of words. Now children start to understand the world around them. Words have meaning and objects have names. Social communication takes off. Children interact with grown-ups and other children. They have a need and desire to play and be with others.

LATER LANGUAGE ACQUISITION

Around three years of age the use of speech and language becomes a socially shared experience. Children can now participate in a conversation where there is a speaker and a listener. The three-year-old child is learning to take turns speaking and listening. When she is doing something, she wants you to watch. How do you know this? You know this because children tell you. Here is an example. Jill gets ready to jump in the puddle. "Mommy, Mommy, look!" Jill waits for Mommy to look in her direction; she wants to know that Mommy is watching before she makes the big splash.

When communication becomes a social experience, children become part of a partnership and share ideas and information. Children are able to begin and end a conversation, and answer questions. They want to be part of this exchange by contributing their thoughts and telling you what is on their mind. At this time of social development, conversations have a purpose. They require children to be able to stay on the topic, and when the topic eventually changes, they need to have the understanding to switch focus and pick up on the new ideas. This is some feat for a three-year-old.

The language delayed child, or child at risk for ASD, does not share the same experiences of language acquisition as typically developing children. Although this is a painful reality, you need to think in different terms. Regardless of your child's chronological age, it will be necessary for you to identify your child's functional age, and begin there. Your challenge right now is to determine your child's language level, and be proactive, in order to help her emerge through this complex barrier.

Last point, if you have any concern that your child is delayed, it is essential that you move forward now. I understand that you may have been waiting because you are giving your child a little more time, but do not delay any longer. As you can see, by three years of age speech and language development is quite sophisticated.

EXPERIENCES TO LANGUAGE

We have seen that from birth through three years of age children go through remarkable, automatic stages of speech and language development. How do children learn to do this?

We know that children understand the world around them even before they are able to talk. Here are three examples.

Jill is a little past her first birthday. She is making lots of sounds, but she is not yet using words. Her mother is cooking and sees Jill about to touch the hot stove, "No!" says her mother. Jill quickly pulls her hand back. A little later Jill is playing with some toys. She is very involved with how the pop-up toy opens. "Jill," her mother calls. Jill looks up and turns her head toward her mother. In the afternoon Jill's mother wants to give her some juice; she asks Jill, "Where is your bottle?" Jill walks over to the table and hands Mother her bottle. Jill and typically developing children respond to words they hear because they already know something about them. Between one and two years of age children understand what they have experienced. They are able to apply their experiences and form images and ideas about them. Then they take the images and ideas they have discovered and file them in their memory bank to be used again and again.

WHAT KINDS OF EXPERIENCES?

Between twelve and sixteen months, children are usually walking. They follow you into the different rooms of your house. They hear you use the words bedroom, sleep, bed, pillow, pajamas, and blanket. They see you use the bedroom experience. They have their own bedroom experience. They see you in the kitchen. They hear you use the words refrigerator, sink, cook, table, and chair. They acquire a kitchen experience, and so on. When you ask typically developing Jill to go to the bedroom and bring the pillow, or go to the kitchen and get the bottle, she can do it. And she can do many more things. She can bring the toy you ask for, and a clean diaper at changing time. She can bring her shoes when getting dressed. At the park she can make a decision and choose the swing instead of the slide. She is able to follow directions: "Jill, put your baby doll in the carriage and cover her with the blanket."

Children delayed in speech and language or at risk for ASD may not be processing the meaning of words the same way as Jill.

Does your twelve- to eighteen-month-old child . . .

Understand the world around him?
Know the names of objects?
Know the function of objects or how to use them?
Follow one- and two-step directions?
Remember information for later use?
Have a desire to speak and socialize?
Focus and pay attention to an object or task?
Use words; is she verbal?
Use more than one word?

HOW DO CHILDREN LEARN WORDS?

Around eighteen to twenty-four months, typically developing children start
to say words. They learn how to assign a specific name to a specific object,
action, or event. Children cannot pick any word; it has to be a word that
everyone who speaks the same language agrees upon. How do children
learn to call a table a table and a chair a chair? Once in a while, why can't
they call a table a chair?

I will explain. Children start off speaking with one word at a time.
This is referred to as the single word stage. Between two and two and
a half years old, they progress to speaking up to two- or three-word
sound bites. By the time they turn three they can speak in phrases,
and short sentences emerge. By five years of age they can speak like
grown-ups! During this time they learn what words mean, what they
represent, how to use them, and where they belong in a sentence. As
children learn more about single words, they begin to expand their use.
From the beginning, these words include all different grammatical uses
such as: nouns for naming, verbs for action, prepositions for places, and
adjectives for descriptions. As time goes on children start to put two words
together, like a noun + a verb, the fish + is swimming. They automatically
know which word goes first, all without a single grammar lesson. The process begins with experiencing an object, its use, and learning that the object
has a name.

Here is an example of how an eighteen-month-old learns the word *table*.
We who speak English all agree that a table is a flat top with four legs. It can
be used as a place to eat, write, or put a lamp. Now, we can talk about tables
because people will understand that we are referring to a particular object,

with a particular function. This results in meaningful communication. If we call a table by any other name, it just won't make sense.

Children will learn about a table from experience. They will sit at a table and eat at a table. They will see dishes and cutlery set on the table, and food brought to the table. Some children may have other table experiences. They may have a small work table and chair where they color or cut. Through all these experiences children are learning the word and its function. Soon the word will be stored in their memory, available to use at other times. As time goes on, children learn that there are other things that are called tables. There are water tables, sand tables, ping-pong tables, pool tables, picnic tables, and even operating tables!

This word experience happens over and over again as children learn more. *Ball*, for example, is one of the early words in a child's single word development. Children learn to roll, throw, catch, kick, and bounce balls. Just like the word *table*, children will gather new experiences and expand what they know about balls. They will discover the baseball, soccer ball, basketball, tennis ball, golf ball, ping-pong ball, and beach ball.

This brings us to an interesting thought. Do children need to see every type of table or ball in the world to know that different-looking tables are still tables and different-looking balls are still balls? Do they need to see every different type of flower in the world to learn that different-looking flowers are still flowers? Did your parents show you every table, every ball, every flower, every "thing" in every category?

The answer is no! Children learn about words and their meanings by making associations about the words. Children learn concepts about the use, function, and image of objects. Then, through experience they realize how a slightly different object matches the function of an object they already know about. So they do not have to see every type of ball to know that a soccer ball and a volleyball are balls. The concept is the same for all: they are round, roll, and can be thrown and bounced. In fact, almost everyone plays with a ball the same way. How about the exceptions? A bowling ball is round but it has holes. Is it still a ball? A football isn't even round, it's oval! And the wiffle ball isn't even a ball! Although these balls are somewhat different, they still have enough characteristics of the image that children know they are still balls.

HOW DOES EXPERIENCE HELP CHILDREN LEARN?

Here is an example of how experience helps children learn. Between two and three years of age children begin to use crayon and paper as a play activity. They scribble, color, and pretend to write like Mommy and Daddy. One day at playgroup, the teacher gives two-year-old, typically developing Jenny a crayon and paper. Jenny thinks, "I can write with this like Mommy and Daddy." A day later instead of crayons, the teacher gives out pencils with lined paper. Again she thinks "um, I can write with this too!" At home, Jenny discovers a container of markers in her sister's room. "Wow," she thinks, "so many things to write with!" The next week Mommy takes Jenny to the park. She gives her a piece of sidewalk chalk. Jenny has never seen or played with chalk. Do you think Jenny is going to take the chalk and use it to dig in the sandbox? I don't think so. Typically developing Jenny is going to think, "Chalk, I can hold it like a pencil or crayon, maybe I can use it the same way. I think I'm going to try writing with this." And she does. From past experiences she uses the chalk like a crayon, and scribbles on the ground in all different colors. Jenny did not have to learn the function and use of a piece of chalk; experience took care of that!

This is what children do. By scanning their memory, they search for past experiences. They search to see if they recognize objects, places, and people. Then they decide if something new matches a concept they already know. By now I hope you agree that children do not need to see every object in the world to know what it is, or how to use it. How do they learn all these words? It can't just be a random plan.

ORGANIZING WORDS INTO CATEGORIES

Children cannot memorize thousands of random words. They need a functional working memory system. The system, when working efficiently, stores images, sounds, ideas, and words. Then, when needed, children recall words that meaningfully relate to the ideas at hand. One of the ways they do this is by organizing large amounts of information into useful categories, filed away in the brain, and stored as knowledge. Then children are able to exchange and share information and knowledge in meaningful ways. They automatically follow the rules of grammar, and put ideas into a sequence of order. They rely on their memory to process, interpret, file, and retrieve information. It almost sounds like I am describing your personal computer.

To do this they create an efficient system of organization by assigning categories to groups of words that share common characteristics. Categories cover large topics, such as land and sea animals, transportation, and sports, furniture, clothing, and foods. Children sort characteristics of different objects into groups. Each group has something in common, and shares some basic trait.

Let's look at foods. There are fruits, vegetables, nuts, grains, meat, fish, and poultry, to name a few. Then each category has its members: fruits have apples, oranges, pears, cherries, and so on. Think of all the dairy products you can list: butter, cheese, milk, and yogurt. How do children do this? Let's use cookies for our example. How do children know that a cookie is a food? How do they know the difference between cookies and soup?

One day Mommy gives Joan a graham cracker. Mommy calls it a cookie and tells her to eat it. It's flat, square, crunchy, sweet, and plain. Joan forms a mental cookie experience. Two weeks later, Mommy gives Joan something round with chocolate chips. Joan thinks, "What is this? It can't be a cookie. It doesn't look like a cookie. Cookies are square!" Mommy says, "cookie." Joan eats the cookie and thinks, "it's flat, crunchy, and sweet, like the other cookie, but it's not square, it's round, it's not plain, it has chips. This is a cookie, too?" Joan goes to the park with Becky. Becky's mommy offers her a cookie. Joan takes the cookie and thinks, "This is a cookie? Two round pieces with white cream inside! It's flat, crunchy, plain, and sweet, but it has cream, and no chips. Although a little confused, Joan is starting to get the point, cookies do not all look the same. Through her experiences she is learning that she can hold a cookie in her hand, it's crunchy, sweet, and tastes yummy. She can eat them and learns cookies are food. In fact, when she starts nursery school she learns something else about cookies. They are also called a snack! Now she can take the larger category of food and file food words into smaller subcategories, cookies and snacks. She learns that cookies can also be a dessert. Joan's brain is filing all this information while creating images about cookies. On Purim, Joan comes to my house. "Would you like a cookie?" "Yes," she replies. I give her a hamentash. Joan looks at this triangle with fruit inside. Can't fool Joan, she knows it's a cookie!

GRAMMAR RULES AND LANGUAGE FOR SINGLE WORDS

When it comes to grammar we think about complicated rules, but there are grammar rules that even apply to single words. When children use these rules appropriately it shows an understanding for language concepts. Here are some examples of how grammar rules are important for language development.

Rule #1: Plurals—Understanding More Than One

Jill is almost three years old. She has two favorite picture books. She shows off her collection and says, "Look, my two book." Jill is demonstrating both a grammar and language error. She needs to learn that more than one object needs to be made plural. It is a concept she will learn and understand through experience. Soon she will realize that book stands for one, but many are books, and she will apply this rule for many cars, cookies, dolls, and anything else where there is more than one. By using the plural form correctly Jill is showing that she understands the concept of quantity, and the difference between one and more than one. It is the beginning of understanding numbers and eventually math. Just by adding the /s/ sound to a single word your child shows an understanding of plurality. One word plus one sound creates a grammar rule. In fact, children Jill's age who have learned this rule, will overgeneralize its use. While pointing to her new sandals Jill says, "Look at my foots!" She has not yet learned the plural for foot is feet, but she has demonstrated an understanding of the rule, for more than one.

Rule #2: Possessive—Understanding Who It Belongs To

Three-year-old Jill is holding her mother's pocketbook and says, "Look, mommy pocketbook." Jill is trying to tell us the pocketbook belongs to her mother. Like plurality Jill will learn and understand this concept through experience. In time she will realize that it is Daddy's book, Grandma's house, and of course, Jill's toy. In fact she will understand the concept of Jill's toy so well she may not allow you to touch it, let alone play with it. Again, one word plus one sound creates a grammar rule. It's amazing how the understanding and use of apostrophe *s* translates into: that object belongs to me.

Rule #3: Tense—Understanding Time

In grammar, the use of tense requires many different forms of a single word. Did you jump, are you jumping, or will you jump? It gets more complicated when the word does not follow rules such as: I am eating dinner or I ate dinner. As we said many times, children learn these rules automatically. How do they do it? Tense is not about learning complicated grammar rules, it's about understanding time. Later in the book you will find fifty words related to time. Just like plurality and possession, tense is a language concept. Children demonstrate their understanding of the concept by translating what they say in the correct grammatical form. Keep in mind that time is a difficult concept for children to master.

Example: Three-year-old Jill went to play at the park yesterday. At this age the concept of yesterday, today, and tomorrow are not really understood. Jill says, "I went with Jane and we play at the park." In time, through experience, Jill will learn that if she did something in the past, she needs to let us know she *played* at the park. In fact, children who have learned this past tense rule will often overgeneralize its use, and say, "I swimmed in the pool." They have not yet learned that the past tense of swim is swam, a more complicated rule about irregular verb forms, but they have demonstrated an understanding of time. Remember, grammar rules can be mastered in one word, or even one sound. When children accomplish this task they have demonstrated a higher level of language understanding.

As you can see, language development is a complex process. By a child's first birthday, communication is intentional and has a purpose. Children begin to use words around eighteen months. From this point, word combinations begin, followed by short phrases and sentences. By three years of age, speech and language becomes a socially shared experience. While playing and interacting children learn about the world. They learn to assign words to objects, people, actions, and events. They organize words into categories and store them in their memory. Expressive language becomes refined and demonstrates mastery of grammatical rules. This mastery begins from the time children learn to connect two words together. Automatically, they know the correct order. In the next chapter I am going to discuss how meaningful two words can be. I will also show you nine examples of two-word combinations. Once your child begins to use words, you will want to encourage her to put two words together. This chapter will show you how.

8

TWO WORDS

Around two years of age, your child will begin to use two words together. She will use a variety of word combinations, expressing her ideas, needs, and wants. You will be amazed to see how much a child can communicate in just two words. Although they may be at a two-word stage in speaking, you will see that the ideas the words represent are quite meaningful. In this chapter I am going to present nine different two-word combinations. I will give you examples of each combination and show you how expressive the words really are.

As your child approaches her second birthday she should begin to use more than one word. Her prewired ability to organize the grammatical rules of English automatically begins. However, her instinct to learn language does not work alone. She needs to hear you and other people around her speak. How do children learn to do this? How do they increase the number of words they use, in a meaningful way? Children have a collection of words in their brain that represent an idea. Their brain also comes equipped with a set of rules that foster word combinations. Children use different combinations of words to talk about their needs and wants. Here are a few examples of two-word combinations that children say. I will use the word *cookie* as the subject word.

good cookie
eat cookie

more cookie
no cookie
that/this cookie

When we understand the context, two-word combinations can have a lot of different meanings. Since children talk about what they are doing or what is happening, let's analyze the possible meanings of these five pairs of words.

Jackie says . . .

"good cookie": Jackie could be eating a cookie or sees a box of cookies that she likes.

"eat cookie": Jackie could mean she is eating a cookie, wants to eat a cookie, or sees Mommy eating a cookie.

"more cookie": Jackie wants another cookie or wants Mommy to have another cookie.

"no cookie": Jackie realizes the cookie box is empty, or she does not want a cookie.

"this/that cookie": Jackie wants a specific cookie, she wants to make a choice.

It is important to take note that in all five examples, with context taken into consideration, Jackie is communicating a lot more than she is able to say. Her thoughts are greater than her words. Now that she has the ability to express a lot of implied information, her communication becomes significantly more effective.

EXCHANGING IDEAS

At this stage, communication also takes on a social dimension. Now parents and children are able to exchange ideas. Children discover that through communication they can satisfy their needs and wants. They can ask for things, and control what they want. Mommy gives Jackie an oatmeal cookie. "No cookie," Jackie says, pushing it away. "This cookie," Jackie says, pointing to the cookie with the chocolate chips. After she eats the chocolate chip cookie Jackie says to Mommy, "more cookie," and she takes another.

Through her exchange with Mommy, Jackie gets the cookie she wants, and when she finishes it, has more. She discovers that communicating gives her power to manage her life. By letting others know what she wants she has the ability to satisfy her desires, and in return, others will fulfill her wishes. Children discover that their requests can be met, not only by their parents but by others around them. The social aspect of communication is developing. With two meaningful words they can engage in a social conversation and begin to build relationships with others. A social conversation is a meaningful exchange between speaker and listener.

WORD COMBINATIONS AND GRAMMAR

Regardless of the mother tongue, two-word combinations need to follow the rules of grammar for the language the child speaks. I am going to show you nine two-word combinations that children begin to use around two years of age. All of these combinations follow the grammatical word order for English. Remember, children are prewired to do this automatically, without a single grammar lesson. You will use these two-word combinations to help advance your child's language development.

Combination #1	**subject + object**
Child says:	*Child may mean:*
"Mommy cookie"	Mommy, I want a cookie.
"Daddy book"	Daddy is holding/reading a book.
"Grandma chair"	Grandma is sitting on the chair.
"Mommy bottle"	Mommy, I want a bottle.
"Mommy diaper"	Mommy, change my diaper.

Combination #2	**action + object**
Child says:	*Child may mean:*
"eat cookie"	Mommy, I'm eating a cookie.
"kick ball"	I can kick a ball.
"drink juice"	I'm drinking juice.
"kiss doll"	Mommy, kiss my doll.
"push car"	Look, I can push the car.

Combination #3	**location + object**
Child says:	*Child may mean:*
"on chair"	My doll is on the chair.
"in box"	The cookie is in the box.
"under table"	The ball is under the table.
"over crib"	The light is over the crib.
"by door"	The carriage is by the door.

Combination #4   **description + object**
Child says: *Child may mean:*
"red ball"   I want the red ball.
"big bear"   The bear is big.
"little mouse"   Look at the little mouse.
"hot soup"   The soup is hot.
"wet diaper"   Change my diaper.

Combination #5   **pronouns + action/object**
Child says: *Child may mean:*
"I go"   I go to the park now.
"You sit"   Telling grandma to sit.
"My toy"   Showing someone his toy.
"He plays"   Telling what the boy is doing.
"She eats"   Telling what the girl is doing.

Combination #6   **action + object**
Child says: *Child may mean:*
"go home"   I want to go home.
"eat cookie"   I want to eat a cookie.
"drive car"   Mommy drives the car.
"cut paper"   I want to cut the paper.
"wash hands"   My hands are dirty.

Combination #7   **action + description**
Child says: *Child may mean:*
"go fast"   The car can go fast.
"come now"   I want Mommy.
"be careful"   This is dangerous.
"be quiet"   Baby is sleeping, or too much noise.
"play later"   Not now.

Combination #8   **subject + verb**
Child says: *Child may mean:*
"Mommy go"   Mommy, I want to go.
"Baby eat"   Look at the baby eating.
"Daddy help"   Daddy is helping Mommy.
"Grandma read"   Grandma is reading a book to me.
"Auntie sing"   My aunt is singing.

Combination #9	**two words that show possession/belongs to**
Child says:	*Child may mean:*
"Mommy shoe"	This is mommy's shoe; it belongs to her.
"Jake bottle"	This is Jake's bottle; it belongs to him.
"Daddy room"	This is daddy's room; it belongs to daddy.
"Man store"	This store belongs to the man; it's his.
"Jack truck"	This toy is Jack's; it belongs to him.

As you can see, there are many ways two words can be expanded to convey meaning. This is the way children start to put words together and expand language. Even though your child may be at risk for language delay, he needs to experience language development the same way as typically developing children. The following two-word combinations are important examples, and you should be familiar with them. These two-word combinations will give you examples of how children begin to put their first words together to expand meaning. You will guide and encourage your child to reach this goal.

8.1. Action + Object = Two Words

	Cookie	Apple	Banana	Pizza	Lollipop
Eat	eat / cookie	eat / apple	eat / banana	eat / pizza	eat / lollipop
Take	take / cookie	take / apple	take / banana	take / pizza	take / lollipop
Want	want / cookie	want / apple	want / banana	want / pizza	want / lollipop
Hold	hold / cookie	hold / apple	hold / banana	hold / pizza	hold / lollipop
Bite	bite / cookie	bite / apple	bite / banana	bite / pizza	bite / lollipop
Chew	chew / cookie	chew / apple	chew / banana	chew / pizza	chew / lollipop
Swallow	swallow / cookie	swallow / apple	swallow / banana	swallow / pizza	swallow / lollipop
Taste	taste / cookie	taste / apple	taste / banana	taste / pizza	taste / lollipop

8.2. Action + Object = Two Words

	Juice	Water	Milk	Tea	Soda
Drink	drink / juice	drink / water	drink / milk	drink / tea	drink / soda
Want	want / juice	want / water	want / milk	want / tea	want / soda
Take	take / juice	take / water	take / milk	take / tea	take / soda
Pour	pour / juice	pour / water	pour / milk	pour / tea	pour / soda
Sip	sip / juice	sip / water	sip / milk	sip / tea	sip / soda
Swallow	swallow / juice	swallow / water	swallow / milk	swallow / tea	swallow / soda

8.3. "More" + Food Word = Two Words; "No More" + Food Word = Two Words

	Apple	Cookie	Banana	Pizza
More	more / apple	more / cookie	more / banana	more / pizza
No More	no more / apple	no more / cookie	no more / banana	no more / pizza

8.4. "More" + Object = Two Words; "No More" + Object = Two Words

	Car	Doll	Truck	Ball	Book
More	more / car	more / doll	more / truck	more / ball	more / book
No more	no more / car	no more / doll	no more / truck	no more / ball	no more / book

8.5. Description/Adjective + Object = Two Words

	Water	Tea	Milk
Cold	cold / water	cold / tea	cold / milk
Hot	hot / water	hot / tea	hot / milk

PERIOD OF IMBALANCE

Understanding and Speaking

There is a time, usually between two and four years of age, when children know and understand a lot more than they are able to say. Each day, through experience, they acquire more and more information about the world; however, their pool of vocabulary is not large enough to match their thought processes. Sometimes children may repeat the sound, "um, um, um," multiple times. This is usually a sign that they are searching for words. As the speaker, children do this to keep you engaged in their conversation, by holding your attention, while they think. This is a typical behavior that disappears as children's conversations become more fluent and their vocabulary increases. There are instances when this type of word searching may continue. This may be a sign of an expressive language delay. Children may not be able to find the words they want to use, or they may not know them. In this chapter you will see how children typically experience this period of imbalance.

You have read how children between twelve and eighteen months of age demonstrate their understanding of the world around them, even before they can speak. You have read how they develop words and categories through new experiences. Around two years of age children advance from single words to two-word combinations. By three years of age children are able to speak in short phrases and simple sentences. What may result is a period of imbalance. Now, children know more than they are able to talk about. They have many ideas, but not enough words. For example, typically developing Jane is three years old. She can sing the entire ABC song, even though she cannot read or write letters. She can sing "Ring around the Rosie" and knows that after she sings, "ashes, ashes," she is supposed to fall down, and she does, even though she does not know what a rosie or ashes are. For now, Jane does not have enough words to talk about the many things she can do and think about, but she is still communicating and socializing.

Now, let's see how typically developing Jake, two and a half years old, interacts at a birthday party. He knows a lot about birthday parties, but he does not have enough words to express his needs and wants. How does he navigate this experience?

Mommy brings Jake to a birthday party. She sits on the side with the other mothers while Jake goes to celebrate. Soon he comes back to Mommy with a birthday hat. He gives Mommy the hat and says, "put on." When the cake comes out Jake joins the other children around the table. He sings the Happy Birthday song in some simplified manner and tries to blow out the candles. Later, he takes a present from the gift table, even though it is not for him, brings it to Mommy, and says, "open, present!" Mommy asks Jake, "Who is the birthday girl?" He correctly points to his cousin and says, "this girl." "What is her name?" asks Mommy. "Julie," replies Jake. Even though his words are limited Jake is communicating enough to express his need, wants, and understanding of the event. From this experience, what do we know about Jake?

Jake appears to understand the experience of a birthday party. He acts appropriately. He wants to wear a party hat like the other kids, he wants a present, and he tries to sing the birthday song. He is successfully processing facts and information that he already knows from previous birthday party experiences which are stored in his memory. Jake will continue to download more information from his memory as he plays with the other children, and he will begin to upload new information as he waits his turn to learn a new game. All this using few words.

IS YOUR CHILD DEVELOPING LIKE JANE AND JAKE?

It is important that your child is developing as I have described. Does your child do the following:

Play like Jane and Jake?
Maintain eye contact?

Play with other children?
Play with toys appropriately?
Talk?
Pay attention?
Follow simple directions?

If you answer no to any of these, have your child evaluated.

This period of imbalance occurs as children know more than they are able to express. We see how children stretch their pool of words to convey their needs and wants. Expressive language and socialization are all part of a networking process in the brain. This process doesn't develop in a vacuum. Memory and attention have a significant role in the process. In the next chapter we are going to look at factors that interfere with communication development.

10

LEARNING, MEMORY, AND ATTENTION

Memory and attention play a significant role in speech, language development, and learning. Different parts of the brain need to work together to achieve mastery of the many different skills children need to acquire. It is necessary for children to establish a solid foundation of basic information that they will build upon throughout their life. In this chapter we will talk about the significant role of learning, memory, and attention.

It would be an unending task if children needed to relearn information every day. Memory makes learning more efficient. Just like a computer saves, stores, and retrieves information, your child's brain is preprogrammed to do the same job. Children have the ability to organize and store what they learn. Then they can recall the information they learned for later use. They do not have to relearn what they already know. Memory also expands as children learn about new objects and events both in and out of their environment. They also use the information they have stored to further expand their knowledge. Functional memory is essential for learning and socialization. How do you know if your child is learning and successfully remembering what he learns?

Here is an example of typically developing three-year-old Jack and how learning and memory work in tandem.

Monday: Jack goes to his playgroup. In the corner he spots blocks. "Blocks," Jack says out loud and goes over to play. He stacks the blocks and makes a tower. The tower falls, Jack rebuilds it. He is happy and enjoys his time in the block corner.

Tuesday: During playtime Jack goes back to the blocks. He does not need to relearn how to make a tower. He remembers what he knows, and continues to play happily.

Wednesday: The teacher spots Jack in the block corner. Noting his interest in blocks, she sits down on the floor to help him expand his experience. She shows Jack how to build a bridge with blocks. They find a toy car. They push the car under the bridge and over the bridge. Jack is now learning new ways to play with blocks. He learns a new word, *bridge*, and expands his vocabulary. He sees what a bridge looks like and how it works. He learns new location words, *under* and *over*, and what they mean in reference to the bridge. Later the teacher shows Jack a picture book about bridges. He sees how bridges go over roads and over water. He discovers, not only can cars go under bridges; boats can go under them too! Through play these new concepts form new memories. This information will last throughout his lifetime, available whenever he calls upon it.

Friday: Jack is in the block corner. Although he needs practice he continues to build towers and bridges. "Beep-beep, toot-toot," he says, as he maneuvers the cars and boats around his construction.

What is Jack showing you? Jack is showing you how efficiently his memory is working. Over time he will amass many new memories. He will not have to relearn what he already knows. Children suspected of ASD do not remember events like Jack. They may remember routine actions, such as using the bathroom and dressing independently, or playing with a toy, but that is not functional memory. Memory plays an important role in language development.

EARLY MEMORY

During the early months of life, babies see objects come and go. Here is an example. You are holding your baby while playing with some toys. First you shake his red rattle. "Shake, shake, shake," you say as you hold the rattle in your baby's hand. Then you take the rubber squeeze toy. "Squeak, squeak, squeak," goes the toy as you press the middle. Is your baby wondering, what happened to the rattle? At this early age, the answer is no. It is as if the rattle disappeared. If Baby cannot see it, it does not exist. How do we know this? Because we have learned that during the early months, babies do not look for objects they can no longer see. If a baby is playing with a ball and it rolls out of sight, they do not try to find it.

As time goes on, your child will become more interested in things. He will have a favorite toy, enjoy his bottle, and drag along his blanket. You will start to notice that as these objects are taken away, your child will look in the direction the objects are moved. Parents play "peek-a-boo" with their children. Babies watch as you cover and uncover your face, saying, "I see you!" They watch objects as you hide them behind your back and suddenly make them reappear. This is entertaining. Your child is paying more attention to what is going on around him. Soon he will begin to discover that an object that is out of sight can come back. This is a significant developmental step for your child. Objects do not disappear. How do we know that your child has made this discovery? We know because children begin to look for objects they no longer can see. The big reward is when they find the ball that rolled behind the chair. Your child now has the ability to think through a series of sequential events. He sees and plays with a ball that rolls out of sight. He looks in the direction where the ball rolled. He was having fun playing with the ball and knows that even though he does not see it, it did not disappear, it still exists. He is now motivated to find it, and he does. Now you can play hiding games with your child. Memory and learning played a role in his success. The brain manages two types of memory, short-term and long-term memory.

SHORT-TERM MEMORY

Before cellular phones, did you ever need to remember a phone number without the luxury of pencil and paper? Remember what you did? You would say the number rapidly over and over in your head; you would listen to your voice repeating the numbers, while staying focused on the task. This constant repetition kept the number active in your short-term memory. As soon as you dialed, the repetitive process ended, and that was the end of the number, gone and forgotten. If you were interrupted, or distracted during this chant of numbers, the number would be gone as well.

REHEARSAL

This vital repetition of information is called rehearsal. The rehearsal phase keeps short-term information active in our mind. Rehearsal is the first step toward making an imprint into memory.

Besides remembering a phone number, there are other daily situations where we need to rehearse short-term information.

Example: You are at a restaurant with a friend, and you need to go outside to make a call. Before you leave you give your order to your friend. "I'll have tuna on toasted rye with lettuce and tomato, a small house salad with oil and vinegar, a decaf coffee, skim milk on the side, and tell the waiter I want the tuna with lite mayo." Your friend has a lot of rehearsing to keep this order active in her short-term memory. Hopefully, she will succeed. Next week you both return to the restaurant. With a quizzical look, you ask your friend, "What did I order last week?" She looks back and says, "I don't remember what I had for breakfast, you expect me to remember what you ordered last week?" You both laugh! Your friend rehearsed your order long enough to store in her short-term memory. Once no longer necessary, her brain said, delete! That short-term order never made it to the long-term memory bank. One of the reasons is because it did not have to. It was not important enough.

Every day we decide what information is important, what we need to keep. What happens when we need to store information in long-term memory? As you read, rehearsal is required to keep information active in our mind, that is step one. Then our brain needs to make a shift from short-term memory to the long-term bank. As a result of chemical and electrical changes taking place in our brain, information gets branded into long-term memory. Over a lifetime, a wealth of information will be filed beyond the short term and permanently stored. Without an efficient memory, building relationships, studying for a career, and daily activities would be almost impossible. Children at risk for ASD have problems with memory.

ATTENTION AND MEMORY

For the child at risk for ASD, the memory process fails before it even begins. This is partly due to an inability to focus and pay attention. Let's look at how paying attention, both listening and looking, has a direct effect on memory and learning. Have you ever spoken to someone, realizing they are not paying attention to a single word you are saying? Have you ever become so annoyed that you yell, "You are not listening to me!" How do we know when someone is not paying attention? We know because when you ask them what you were saying, they cannot tell you. We sense the importance of attention. If we didn't, we would not lose our patience, become upset, and feel like we wasted our time. It frustrates us. It is a problem when someone is consistently not paying attention.

When children are not paying attention, it is as if they are not there. So the child who is not attending at home, in school, during the movie, while listening to the story, or watching the baseball game will not know what was said, what was taught, or what just happened. They cannot recall information from their memory because, quite simply, it never made it there. It was lost just like the telephone number and the tuna fish sandwich. Attention is also affected by poor eye contact and disruptive behavior.

ASD AND ATTENTION

The child at risk for ASD has significant challenges with attention. He appears unable to focus long enough on what he is hearing, seeing, or doing, so he doesn't know what is going on. Some children at risk are easily distracted and impulsive, unable to control their maladaptive behavior. Others have sensory issues that interfere with attention. Sometimes parents feel their child is ignoring them, or they worry that they may have a hearing loss. Some children at risk may selectively pay attention, others cannot, and some children tune out because they don't understand what is happening. Regardless, these are all barriers, interfering with attention, memory, and learning.

Does your child demonstrate the following behaviors that interfere with attention?

Tantrums
Self-injurious behavior
Self-stimulating behavior such as rocking or spinning
Throwing objects or using them inappropriately such as tapping with a
    spoon
Hitting others
Constantly on the go
Disinterest
Acting as if you or others are not there

If you answer yes to any of these questions it's important to seek advice and have your child evaluated.

ASD AND MEMORY

Children at risk for ASD, especially low functioning children on the spectrum, have severe difficulty with memory. Memory interference begins from the first step, by a breakdown in rehearsal. As a result, information does not have a chance to remain active in short-term memory in order to be transferred into long-term memory storage. The names for objects and events cannot be transferred into the permanent storage file. This is because the information does not remain active to make the memory shift from short-term to long-term memory. This is one reason why it is so difficult for the child at risk to retain what they have learned. This is why children at risk need to relearn information.

Memory and Your Child

Does your child remember objects he has played with?
Does your child remember places he has been?
Does he remember people and faces?
Does he show recognition of past experiences?
Does he look for things that move out of sight?

There are many ways to short-circuit memory. It may begin with a lack of attention. What causes this to happen? One cause is an inability to concentrate. This may be due to a biochemical or neurological disorder, too many distractions, or selective attention. For the child with ASD, all of these are possible reasons.

BIOCHEMICAL/NEUROLOGICAL DISTURBANCE

ASD is a neurodevelopmental disorder. The mechanism of the brain responsible for attention, focus, and memory is not working the same way as it does for typically developing children. These are ways the process is affected:

blocking: information is not getting into the memory system
distortion: the brain is not interpreting what it sees and hears accurately
disorganization: information is not being filed with a strategy
retrieval: information cannot be accessed

ASD AND VISUAL ATTENTION MEMORY

A failure in visual memory will interfere with remembering or linking faces to people, understanding facial expressions, and recalling places and objects. In addition, some children at risk for ASD have selective visual attention. This is when a child is overly focused on a detail or part of an object or event. It is as if they zoom in like a camera and select a feature to spotlight, while at the same time losing sight of the whole.

Example: Jerry is sitting on the floor with a few cars and trucks. There is also a make-believe parking lot and road signs, a lot of opportunity for creative play. Jerry chooses to play with the cars and begins to spin one of the wheels. He plays with the same car, spinning the same wheel, and does not stop until you take it away. He focuses on the wheel to the exclusion of all the other toys in his reach. In fact, it appears as if he does not even see or know that the other toys are around. Although Jerry has played with toy cars before, he has not been able to file a functional or meaningful image in order to play more appropriately. He has not made any new discoveries. As a result, he is unable to retrieve useful information from past experiences. This is because he does not have any stored in his memory. Jerry's selective visual hyperattention is not productive.

Jerry is unwilling or unknowing to shift his attention. This inability to shift his visual attention is not only related to objects. He does not shift his attention to acknowledge if you, a relative, or a friend comes into the room, nor does he turn his head to look in your direction. In addition, Jerry becomes explosive and throws a tantrum when he is interrupted from his ritual behavior.

Here is another example of selective visual attention. I was working with a high functioning mainstream ten-year-old boy diagnosed with ASD. I gave him a cartoon-style picture of a farmer harvesting his vegetable garden. Next to the farmer is a *basket* partially filled with carrots he just picked. A boy waves his hand as he passes by the farmer. The assignment was for the student to look at the picture and write a story about it. Here are the results:

He titled his story, "The Boy Who Lost His Bucket."

The entire one-page story was about the basket, which my student called a *bucket*. He wrote about the *bucket* over and over:

"Who lost a *bucket*?" No one answered, so he took it. He started to use the *bucket* for everything. One day he woke up went to the field to get his *bucket* but he didn't see his *bucket*.

My student was so focused on the *bucket* that he lost sight of the whole. There wasn't any development about the farmer harvesting the vegetables, the garden, or even the boy passing by. In addition, the basket belonged to the farmer not the boy. The title, *The Boy Who Lost His Bucket*, does not have any relevance to the picture. My student was hyperfocused on one object—the *bucket*—and couldn't deviate from the theme.

Besides this highly focused selective visual memory, some children at risk also demonstrate supergeneralized and rote memory.

ASD AND GENERALIZED AND ROTE MEMORY

Many children at risk for ASD are able to learn generalized functions of objects and actions. These tasks are, for the most part, imitated with little understanding. The child knows how to brush his teeth, open a juice box and straw, sit on chairs, and go to sleep in his bed. But he does not use words to name the objects he is interacting with, nor does he have ideas about what he is doing. If you ask him a question he cannot answer.

Besides generalized memory disorder, some children have a strong ability to remember large chunks of information like the dialogue from a video, parts of a movie screenplay, or commercials. This is called rote memory. Rote memory is the ability to memorize or remember information word for word with accurate recall. Again, this is accomplished with little understanding of the verbatim script. In light of what appears to be an exceptional memory, this child may not be able to remember simple tasks, people, or names of familiar objects.

Here is an actual verbatim example of rote memory. I was so amazed by this event that I rushed to write down every word.

One afternoon, soon after the first Pixar movie *Cars* came out, a boy I was working with arrived for our usual therapy session holding a Batman Band-Aid.

I asked, "Where did you get that Batman Band-Aid?"

He replied: "My grandfather gave it to me."

But that was not the end of the conversation; he continued:

"From Disney Pickstar movie, [he meant Pixar]

Cars

From Disney Pickstar movie,

Cars

The Pickstar movie,

> *Cars* is available on DVD
> From Disney Pickstar movie,
> *Cars*
> You know the red car
> blue car
> green car
> It makes the Pickstar and it's an animation.
> I saw a bald eagle when I came here at a high school yard
> To protect and serve the galaxy
> The good Lego Batman experience
> XPD full powered."

At this point, I stopped him. If I did not he would have happily continued this one-sided, self-absorbed monologue. We can agree, great memory, but not functional, meaningful, or useful.

INCONSISTENCY WITH ASD AND MEMORY

There is a lot of inconsistency when it comes to memory, language development, and ASD. Autism is referred to as a spectrum disorder because there is a broad difference in levels of functioning between children. The terminology is quite polarized. Children are often classified as high or low functioning, verbal or nonverbal. Little is described in between. This should give you an example of how wide the ability range spans. For an example, let's look at math and memory.

MATH AND MEMORY

Some children diagnosed with ASD can remember remarkable math facts; however, when it comes to math problem-solving skills, they cannot apply the math they know.

Example: Judy has four cookies and Jen has two cookies. How many cookies do they have all together? Or Judy and Jen have six cookies all together. If they each eat one, how many cookies will be left? Although the child is quite capable of adding 4 + 2, or subtracting 6 − 2, he cannot solve the cookie problem. He can work with numbers but he cannot interpret mathematical words. He does not understand that "all together" requires addition and "how many left" requires subtraction. The story line of the problem is too confusing, making the problem too complex. This is because children at risk have significant difficulty processing the words they hear. Simply, they do not understand the message.

As we have read, memory and attention play a major role in childhood development. Memory begins early, during babies' first months, and hopefully will serve throughout their lifetime. Building memories requires the ability to focus and pay attention over a period of time. Memory also requires the ability to screen out distractions. Learning is dependent on the brain's ability to successfully manage these tasks. Sometimes children appear to be paying attention, but they don't understand what they are hearing. Hearing is within normal limits, but for some reason the message is confusing. In the next chapter we are going to talk about auditory processing disorder, when the brain doesn't understand what it hears.

11

AUDITORY PROCESSING DISORDER

Auditory processing disorder may be a significant component of delayed language development and ASD. For children who are language delayed, it is possible that they do not understand what they hear. The message may be too fast, or too complex. For children at risk for ASD, auditory processing is a significant obstacle. As a characteristic symptom, the part of the brain responsible for encoding the auditory message is severely impaired. In this chapter I will discuss the impact of auditory processing.

An auditory processing disorder is an inability for the brain to understand and accurately interpret the message it hears. Hearing the message is fine. The problem is understanding what is heard. As we saw with math, a child may be able to add or subtract numbers, but once the example is presented in a problem-solving format, the message becomes too complex to interpret, and the ability to understand declines. The brain cannot process the information. Children at risk for ASD have considerable difficulty processing auditory information, information which is heard. One of the reasons they seem so detached and unresponsive is because they do not understand what they hear. To make matters worse, background noise, speaking quickly, and using too many words complicates the situation even more.

A great way to understand what is happening when your child is having difficulty with auditory processing is to compare it to a popular magician's trick. The magician starts off with a big black top hat, empty, of course, and his wand. He shows you there is nothing up his sleeve, waves a colorful handkerchief before you, and proceeds to put it in the hat. He waves his wand, and to everyone's surprise, out comes a rabbit! What goes in is not what comes out. And that is what is happening with the messages your child hears. The information is heard, but it is not understood. What you are saying is not what your child is interpreting. By carefully listening to your child's response, you will be able to understand what he thought you meant.

In order for you to understand auditory processing confusion, I am going to give you a simple example of how the brain misinterprets what it hears.

Example: Mommy takes three-and-a-half-year-old Jane to the produce [fruit and vegetable] store.

Mommy asks Jane, "Where do fruits and vegetables come from?"

Jane replies, "apple."

The expected answer would be farm. Fruits and vegetables come from the farm. Apple is surely not the correct answer; produce does not come from an apple. Let's analyze Jane's response.

It is possible, if Jane lives in the city, that she may not know about farms. She may not have any experience about where produce is grown. OK, I will agree with that, but let's pretend that Jane does live in a big city, and has no farm experience. She still could have given a more accurate answer. Jane could have said that fruits and vegetables come from a truck, because she saw produce taken off the truck. To her that is where produce comes from. Or she could have said that fruits and vegetables come from a box, because she has had the experience of seeing produce taken out of a box and put on display for sale.

Why would I accept these two answers from a city child, when a truck and a box have nothing to do with a farm? It is because both answers demonstrate that Jane understands the question. She processed that she was being asked a *where* question. From her experience the truck or the box demonstrates her understanding of where. She answered with a location word, a place.

So, explain why her answer, apple, is wrong. Apple is wrong because Mommy did not ask Jane to tell her the name of a fruit. If she did, then apple would be correct. She asked Jane where fruits and vegetables come from. The operative word in the question is *where*. Jane needed to extract the word where, and rapidly process that her answer needs to be a place. Jane did not process the word *where*. More likely she focused on the word *fruit*, and told her mother the name of a fruit.

Although this explanation is quite simplified, it demonstrates auditory processing confusion: a misunderstanding of what is heard. This is what happens when children cannot process the message accurately. In fact, it is common for children to take what they heard last, or extract one word and focus on that part. They lose sight of the message in its entirety. That is what Jane did. She heard fruits and vegetables, zoned in on fruit, and answered "apple."

ASD AND AUDITORY PROCESSING DISORDER

Children at risk for ASD have serious problems processing auditory information. The part of their brain responsible for interpreting what it hears is not functioning the way it does for typically developing children.

Here is an example of a child I see in therapy, diagnosed with ASD. He has significant problems with auditory processing. Look at how he responds to the questions.

> Jake comes to therapy and starts to play with a toy plane.
> Barbara: "What is this?" [pointing to the plane]
> Jake: "wagon"; "helicopter"
> Barbara: "airplane"
> "Where does it fly?"
> Jake: "in the sky"
> Barbara: "What is this?" [holding the airplane and asking again]
> Jake: "fly in the sky"
> Barbara: "What is this?" [still holding the airplane]
> Jake: "in the sky"

Let's analyze Jake's responses. Jake is having difficulty processing the questions, and recalling words that he knows. He cannot find the word for airplane; however, he has an image in his mind of something that can move. He tries wagon. He pauses while looking at the airplane, and recalls an image that planes belong in the sky. He rejects wagon. Wagons do not fly in the sky. This cannot be a wagon. He pauses again and says helicopter. Although he could not find the word *airplane*, he did choose a word within the category of things that fly in the sky. This is a big accomplishment for Jake. Look at all the layers of operations he does to find a somewhat relevant answer.

To eliminate frustration I tell him that the toy he is holding is an airplane. To expand the concept of the airplane I ask, "Where does it fly?" Now Jake has the airplane in hand and correctly processes the question, "in the sky."

"Great job!" but I still want Jake to use the word for airplane.

I ask him again, "What is this?" while pointing to the toy.

"In the sky," he answers.

"What is this?" I ask again.

"Fly in the sky," he responds. Jake is very proud of himself. He knows air-planes and helicopters fly in the sky. Regardless of the question, he answers "in the sky" over and over again. He is not processing that the question has changed. This is called perseveration.

PERSEVERATION: UNCONVENTIONAL VERBAL BEHAVIOR

Jake is excited that he knows the plane flies in the sky. He is so happy to answer my question, but Jake is starting to perseverate. Perseveration is the repetition of a word, phrase, or question said over and over without relevance. He is not focusing on the question. He hears my voice, but he is not processing the change in words. Jake is stuck on his answer; he is un-able to switch channels. Besides not processing the question, Jake is now perseverating. Perseveration is not the only unconventional verbal behavior typical for ASD. Echolalia is an unconventional verbal behavior as well. I will explain.

ECHOLALIA: UNCONVENTIONAL VERBAL BEHAVIOR

Besides using perseverative speech, Jake repeats what he hears. Instead of answering questions, Jake will repeat them. This repetition is called echo-lalia. It is a common form of unconventional verbal behavior for the child with ASD. Your child may echo what he has just heard, or what he has heard in the past. Although typically developing children may experience a period of echolalia, it is short-lived and decreases as expressive and social language develops. For the child with ASD, echolalic speech occurs more frequently and may last for a long time. It appears there are many reasons why children use echolalic speech. It may be because they don't know what to say, or it is an automatic response to what they hear, or they think it's what you want them to say. In my clinical experience I believe that many of the children who repeat what I say do it because they believe it is what I want them to do. Some of the children I work with appear proud after they repeat my words. Of course, we don't really know why, but it may be due, in part, to the obstacles facing language acquisition and social language development. However, echolalia in children diagnosed with ASD is considered a positive step toward the emergence of language development in the future.

If your child is verbal, write down what he says, and his responses to questions. Recording his expressive language is important and valuable. It allows you to analyze the vocabulary he actually uses. Based on his responses, you can determine if he understands and processes the information he hears appropriately. If his answers are not appropriate, you can identify what he does not understand and make that a goal to work on. If your child uses perseverative or echolalic speech, or continuously asks questions, write them down, too. You may learn that these speech samples are attempts by your child to communicate.

Use the following chart to help record samples of your child's expressive language. Make multiple photocopies and organize them in a binder. Take the binder when you are out with your child. Fill in the date, your child's age, and the context or place where you are recording your child's expressive language. Record what she says, or list words she is using.

LANGUAGE PROCESSING CHART

Date:
Age:
Context: park, pizza store, other
Questions, responses, child's words
1.
2.
↓ [continue]

PROCESSING WORDS FOR UNDERSTANDING

As you can see, words need to be processed accurately. Here are examples of important "wh" words your child needs to be able to process and understand. Children at risk for ASD have significant difficulty understanding these *wh* words. They are very important for language development, processing, and comprehension. Without an understanding of these words it will be very difficult to break through the language barrier of ASD.

Who: refers to a person.
What: refers to a name or a description.
Where: refers to a place.
When: refers to time.
What is he/she doing: refers to an action.
How: refers to the description of an action.

ANALYSIS OF THE *WH* WORDS

How are these words processed?

Who gave you the doll?	Grandma	person
What is the doll wearing?	a dress	name
What color is the dress?	red	description
Where is the doll?	in the carriage	place
When does your doll go to sleep?	at night	time
What is your doll **doing?**	drinking her bottle	action
How does your doll feel?	happy	description

Here is an analysis of the above *wh* word examples:

Who gave you the doll? It could be Grandma, the teacher, or a friend.
   For a *who* question the answer must be a person—a common or
   proper noun.
What is the doll wearing? It could be a dress, shoes, or a hat. The answer
   needs to be a word in the category of clothing—a noun.
What color is the dress? Must be a color that describes the dress—an
   adjective.
Where is the doll? The answer could be in the carriage, here, in the crib.
   It must be a location/place—preposition word.
When does your doll go to sleep? It could be at night, after her bath, or
   7:00, but the word must be a time.
What is your doll **doing?** It could be drinking, playing, running. It must
   be an action—a verb.
How does your doll feel? It could be happy, hungry, sleepy. It must de-
   scribe feelings—an adverb.

Remember, the answer must complement the question word, so if someone asks you, "When do you exercise?" your answer could be in the morning, before bed, or never . . . but it cannot be zumba!

How can you determine how auditory processing impacts on your child's language delay? Try to identify what he does not understand. You will determine this through *wh* questions as illustrated above. Although a challenging goal, processing these concepts is essential for language comprehension.

Look at the figure on the next page. Use the *wh* pictures as a guide. Ask your child different *wh* questions. This will help you determine your child's understanding of these important words. If your child is just beginning to use language, start with *who, what,* or *where* questions. Keep in mind that *when,* a concept of time, is more abstract and complex to process. In part five, I will talk about the importance of using picture schedules. You will see how routines and picture schedules help with understanding time and sequence.

Auditory processing is the key to understanding the messages that are heard. A lot of factors contribute to successful processing. Paying attention is necessary; otherwise, it is as if you never heard what is being said. Maintaining an environment that is without, or has minimal, distractions is important. Distractions may be noise, clutter, interruptions, temperature, or visual overstimulation. In the next chapter I am going to make suggestions about how to simplify the message when speaking to a child with a processing disorder.

WHO

WHAT

WHERE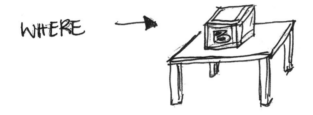

WHEN

12

WAYS TO SPEAK TO YOUR CHILD
WITH A PROCESSING DISORDER

Many of us do not realize how many words we use to get our point across, or how quickly we speak. For the child with a processing disorder the complexity and speed of a message can make it impossible to be understood. In this chapter I am going to present some suggestions about modifying what you say, and how you say it.

Speaking in your usual conversational style may be too complex for your child to understand. You will need to simplify how you speak. Presume your child does not understand what you are saying until you know she does. To stay focused on this goal pretend she does not understand English. We make a lot of adjustments when we talk to someone who does not know our language. Make the same types of adjustments when speaking to your child. This is what I suggest:

- Speak slowly.
- Use a minimal number of words to make your point.
- Use gestures, pictures, or objects to help communicate; visual cues are important.
- Show your child where things are at home and outside.
- Tell your child the names of things.
- Tell your child who people are.

- Tell your child what you are doing.
- Maintain eye contact to encourage attention and focus.

There are many ways to modify a message. Remember, your child is having difficulty with understanding. Reduce the number of words, slow down the speed, and use visual and hands-on experiences. These techniques may help your child begin to understand the world around her. Once she understands the world better, it will be less scary and confusing. Besides understanding words, your child also needs to understand the cues of social language. Social language is referred to as pragmatic language. In the next chapter I will talk about pragmatic language disorder, which is another characteristic symptom of ASD.

⓭

SOCIAL LANGUAGE

Social language is a complex function of communication, necessary to build relationships with others. For children at risk for ASD, social language is seriously disordered. It is a significant handicap that will present lifelong challenges. In this chapter, I will discuss pragmatic language and its disorders.

What is pragmatic language? Simply stated, pragmatic language is the social use of language. I call it the psychology of language. Pragmatic language is the ability and desire for a child to do the following:

- Express his needs and wants: "I'm hungry; I want a cookie."
- Ask questions: "How does this work?"
- Discover that communication provides a sense of positive control: "I want to play."
- Learn to be assertive through words: "No!"
- Exchange ideas through social interaction and conversation:
  - Mommy: "What do you want to eat?"
  - Child: "pizza," if your child responds with "eating," this response is inappropriate.
- Stay on the topic:
  - Mommy: "What are you building?"
  - Child: "I like balloons." This response is irrelevant.

Pragmatic language is also when the speaker thinks about the words she chooses to say, and how she says them, as well as considering the feelings of the listener and the circumstances at the time. Carefully choosing the right words to say is also a function of pragmatics.

ASD AND PRAGMATIC LANGUAGE

Most professionals agree that the greatest impact of ASD is the breakdown in the use of communication. In the most severe cases the child diagnosed with ASD appears to lack the need and desire to speak. Many children in this category may remain nonverbal throughout their lifetime. However, autism is a spectrum disorder. Not all children with autism are nonverbal. There is a range of ability from high functioning to low functioning. What is unique about ASD, compared to other developmental disorders, is that early diagnosis, early intervention, and intensive ongoing therapy can have a significant impact on reducing or even eliminating the deficits that distinguish the disorder. What separates higher functioning children diagnosed with ASD from less able children is their language development and social communication skills. Although many children with ASD attend mainstream schools, pragmatic skills remain the most challenging obstacle.

PRAGMATIC LANGUAGE: HOW IT IMPACTS ON HIGH FUNCTIONING CHILDREN WITH ASD

High functioning children diagnosed with ASD think differently than typically developing children. Here are some characteristics of high functioning children with ASD:

- Think in concrete terms
- Interpret literally what people say
- Have difficulty with idioms and metaphors
- Do not understand jokes
- Are confused by multiple-meaning words such as weak/week
- Have difficulty with reading comprehension since they cannot put themselves in the place of the characters
- Have difficulty reading people's faces and feelings
- Are socially inappropriate; ignore the feelings and needs of other children around them

- Are impulsive
- Are egocentric
- Lack social manners, such as offering your seat to an older person or waiting for a guest to take their food first

WHY DON'T KIDS PLAY WITH ME?

By five years of age, typically developing children use language like adults, but their social language is different. Kids talk about toys, the latest animated characters, and candy. Grown-ups talk about jobs, the economy, and global affairs. Children with ASD often do not know what is appropriate to talk about. They may have difficulty staying on a topic and misjudge their own actions. Knowing what to talk about is a very important part of communication. Disordered social communication significantly impairs the ability to develop appropriate friendships and relationships. As a result, kids with ASD often do not understand why other children may not want to play with them. They do not understand that what they are doing may be judged by their peers as inappropriate.

UNDERSTANDING FEELINGS

Pragmatic skills are about reading other people. It's about empathy and taking into consideration what others are thinking and feeling. If someone is crying you would expect a friend to act differently than if he were laughing. If someone is angry you would act differently than if he was happy. You need to be able to read and understand someone's feelings, emotions, and facial expressions to socially "fit in"—children with ASD have significant difficulty with this aspect of communication.

- We can agree that calling 911 is different than calling a friend.
- Words used at a birthday party are different than words used in a hospital.
- Your voice and loudness at a baseball game is different than in a library.

All these social skills are an essential part of therapy. Through role-playing, pictures, and hands-on experiences, children with ASD need to be taught how to react to different situations.

I have worked with many high functioning children with ASD who attend mainstream schools. I am still amazed at the way they interpret information. One adorable high functioning nine-year-old comes to mind. Here is a sample of three short conversations I had with her.

We were working on a math problem that was too complex for her to understand. "Let me show you," I said, and motioned for her to give me her pencil to highlight some important words to help. Suddenly, she became angry with me, "Why are you taking my pencil? I'm not finished yet." She completely misread my gesture. I only wanted to use the pencil for a moment to help.

On another occasion, my tote bag was on the chair she usually sat on in the therapy room. When we entered the room, I was carrying her heavy book bag. "Your bag is on my chair," she said in an irritable manner. I needed to put down her heavy books before I could remove my bag. Again she impatiently said, "Your bag is on my chair; when are you going to move it?" She could not project that I needed to put her books down first. This very sweet, adorable child became somewhat belligerent at what she believed to be my audacity for not removing my bag from her chair. Her goal was to sit down, period. Her extreme tunnel vision was void of interpreting the cause-and-effect situation that was occurring right before her. If this happened in school with another child, especially in a mainstream middle school, she may have caused an unnecessary argument if not worse.

The same nine-year-old comes to therapy directly from school. Her mother usually provides a snack and reminds her to eat it. On this occasion it was a few slices of apple. Minutes before the session ended, my next student arrived and waited his turn to take her seat. Then we heard her mother arrive. As usual she packed up her books, put on her coat, and was ready to leave, but then she realized she didn't eat the apple. "Wait, I didn't eat my apple," and proceeded to go back to the table, with her coat on, to eat it. "You will have to wait to eat your apple later," I said. She looked at me with a confused look on her face and said, "Why?" She couldn't understand why she could not eat the apple, nor could she understand that the session was over, her mother had arrived to pick her up, and it was the next child's turn.

As children on the spectrum grow up, these social mistakes become quite problematic, resulting in a social communication disability. In the next chapter, I am going to talk about the high price children and adolescents diagnosed with Asperger syndrome pay for their inability to read people and situations.

(14)

ASPERGER SYNDROME

Some kids are called goofy, weird, or nerdy by their peers. There is a reason why these children are called names. They are socially handicapped on the high functioning end of the autism spectrum. In this chapter, I am going to discuss Asperger syndrome and how it impacts relationships with others.

Children diagnosed with high functioning ASD are given the diagnosis of Asperger syndrome (AS). AS is a social and communication disability. Unlike autism, characteristics of AS are as follows:

- Speech and language develops at the expected age.
- Children are aware of others and their environment.
- Children demonstrate special interests that may be unusual.
- They have a desire to socialize yet social judgment may be poor.
- Most significantly misunderstand others, resulting in rejection and social isolation.

As the child with AS becomes older and moves into adolescence and adulthood, the social stigma can become more complex. Misreading the cues of others is common, since the young adult is unable to monitor and understand facial expressions, body language, and the context of many social situations. The young adult is unable to monitor and understand the cues of others. An added barrier that is difficulty with abstract conversation. Continuous and persistent discussions never seem to come to a point. Conversations are filled with endless facts and details. The listener becomes annoyed. Friends may avoid further contact. The young adult is left frustrated with the feeling of being unwanted.

WHEN IS ASPERGER SYNDROME DIAGNOSED?

AS is usually not diagnosed until around three years of age. This is because spoken language usually develops normally within the early childhood years. Single words develop between eighteen months to two years of age, two-word responses and short phrases between two and three years of age. During this period there is usually no significant delay. Formal language skills are underway. The rules of spoken grammar are falling into place, and vocabulary is steadily increasing.

WHAT HAPPENS AFTER THREE YEARS OF AGE?

After three years of age language development takes a significant and obvious change in development. The most apparent change is in social interaction. Suddenly, the child starts to develop unusual and intense limited interests. The child will begin to talk continuously about a topic that has no relevance or interest to anyone except him.

Language may become perseverative, which means words or ideas are repeated over and over again, just like my ten-year-old student who kept writing about the *bucket.* Another example is the child who excessively weaves the lyrics of a theme song or jingle into her ongoing conversation.

MISSING THE CUES: THE SOCIAL FAILURE

Unfortunately, the child diagnosed with AS is oblivious to the listener's feelings. Eventually the listener will begin to look away, stop paying attention, or show facial expressions of annoyance. The child is unable to interpret these nonverbal cues and will continue with his repetitive, verbose, one-sided conversation without "reading" the reaction of the listener. This lack of social judgment is a major deficit of AS and may lead to social isolation and rejection.

Asperger syndrome will bring lifelong social challenges. Role-playing, acting out behaviors in a variety of social settings, and even creating a picture book of socially appropriate actions will be significantly important for the child with AS. In addition, establishing an ongoing relationship with a social worker or psychologist will be important for emotional support and guidance. Children with AS will need to learn how to make decisions in different settings. In the next chapter, I am going to talk about how children learn to make decisions, troubleshoot problems, control impulsive behavior, and project consequences.

15

HOW THE BRAIN WORKS

Autism is a broad-based neurodevelopmental disorder where the brain is not processing and networking information like the typically developing child. There have been many theories about the cause of ASD, from external factors such as vaccinations to biological factors linked to genetics. For now, what we do know is that ASD is a language-based disorder that affects cognitive, social, and emotional development. We have discussed how language, processing, attention, and memory impact on the child with ASD. But how does the child with autism think? How does the brain respond to this task? In this closing chapter of part one, I am going to discuss theory of mind (TOM) and executive function disorder (EFD), both linked to how the brain works.

THEORY OF MIND

Theory of mind is a significantly important human function directly related to social skills. Simply, it is the ability to understand the intentions and emotions of others and knowing how to act. For children, it's the ability to play well with others, understand why a child is crying, and getting help if a child seems sick or hurt. Children do this through experience, responsible parenting, maturity, and maybe even instinct. The ability to share, empathize, and make friendships is key for the social success of a child. These social qualities will not only be evident when children play together, but even when they are engaged in pretend play by themselves.

Difficulty understanding others is a core feature of ASD and appears to be a universal deficit and challenge. Research shows that typically developing children between three and four years of age have ideas about how their brain works. They are able to identify the physical job of the brain, such as it makes you move, and they are able to identify mental functions of the brain, such as dreaming and keeping secrets. At four years of age, children diagnosed with ASD have been able to identify physical jobs of the brain but couldn't associate abstract functions. In addition, children with ASD have difficulty with projecting what others may think; they can only process an event from what *they* know. Between four and six years of age, typical children can express their emotions about how they feel and how they expect to feel. So the child is happy about the birthday present she got and excited waiting for the present. These same emotional feelings are not typical for the child with ASD.

It is possible that your child at risk will face lifelong challenges understanding others. Through counseling, role-playing, and viewing pictures, children with ASD can learn about different social behaviors and appropriate responses. Before taking your child to a party, restaurant, or on a trip, it's a good idea to let her know in advance where you are going and why, what it will be like, what she should expect, and how she should react. I don't suggest this discussion on your way to the occasion. It should be enough in advance to allow you to show her pictures, possibly visit, or even role-play the upcoming event.

Lastly, children with ASD also have difficulty with gaze direction and visual attention. Gaze direction is movement of the eyes. We spend a lot of time looking into people's eyes. We do this because by watching the gaze direction of someone's eyes, you can know if they are thinking about something, gazing at something of interest, or gazing at something they want. The child with ASD has difficulty with interpreting gaze direction. In fact, when looking at faces, which is related to visual attention, more concentration is spent looking at the mouth than the eyes. Here lies the problem: since emotional information is conveyed through the eyes, the information is probably not noticed. Although it will be important and necessary to work with your child using hands-on and visual experiences, picking up on what someone's eyes are telling them will be a challenge.

Now that I've talked about theory of mind, the last area I want to present is executive function. I refer to the brain's executive function as the *captain of the ship*.

EXECUTIVE FUNCTION DISORDER

The brain is a well-organized organ of neural pathways, a network where information is broadcasted through different regions. The circuitry, when working at its best, integrates information from different regions and works harmoniously. The brain does a miraculous job of simultaneously carrying out multiple functions. These include multitasking, controlling impulses, staying focused, paying attention, making judgments by screening out irrelevant information, blocking out distractions, monitoring performance while achieving goals, and keeping what is necessary in active memory.

Children with ASD have difficulty with executive function, and are often diagnosed with executive function disorder. Simply stated, they lack a captain. The part of the brain responsible for this overwhelming *managerial* job is not functioning effectively. In addition, executive function plays a critical and necessary role in language development and language processing. For children with ASD, both language development and processing are the central components of the disorder, therefore executive function must be part of the disorder as well.

What are the characteristics of executive function disorder? Executive function disorder is the inability to pay attention, focus, stay on topic, inhibit distractions, consider the feelings of others, control impulses, maintain working memory, shift attention, and eliminate repetitive behaviors. In other words, executive function is all about cognitive, social, and behavioral growth and development. With early intervention and the support of a behavioral therapist or ABA (applied behavior analysis) specialist, you will work hard to improve your child's language function, knowledge about the world, and distracting behavior. In turn, she will develop language skills, learn how to harness her behavior, and better understand social cues. With a team approach, trained professionals, and repetition, hopefully you will be able to help her break through the barrier of autism.

PART ONE SUMMARY

In this section we have talked about speech and language and how ASD impacts on its development. In the next sections we will talk about practical ways to set up your home, what materials to have, playing with realistic toys, and ways to stimulate your child's speech, language, and social development.

Part Two

WORKING WITH
YOUR CHILD

INTRODUCTION

I can remember the frustration of not being able to talk at age three.
This caused me to throw many a tantrum. I could understand what people said to me, but I could not get my words out. It was like a big stutter,
and starting words was difficult. My first few words were very difficult to
produce and generally had only one syllable, such as "bah" for ball. . . .
I can remember logically thinking to myself that I would have to scream
because I had no other way to communicate. Tantrums also occurred
when I became tired or stressed by too much noise, such as horns going
off at a birthday party. My behavior was like a tripping circuit breaker.
One minute I was fine, and the next minute I was on the floor kicking
and screaming like a crazed wildcat.

—Temple Grandin

These are the words and early childhood memories of Temple Grandin
from her 1995 autobiography, *Thinking in Pictures: My Life with Autism.*
Grandin has become the voice for those who share her life experience.
Firsthand, she lets us in on the "unimaginable" world of autism. So it is no
wonder that working with children at risk for ASD remains uncharted terri-
tory. What is most profound is that, except for Grandin, few have been able
to tell us what it's all about. Therefore, it is for this reason that I begin part
two with her moving words.

Paying heed to Grandin's insight, we learn about her chaotic, terror-filled, fearful childhood, and how her acquisition of language became "an almost miraculous power by which she might gain some mastery of herself." Her development of language and understanding would ultimately further her contact with others and enable some connection to the world. So it appears only practical to follow her lead. She tells us that children on the spectrum need to learn in pictures, that learning needs to be concrete and visual. That's what the rest of this book is about, translating our words into concrete pictures and meaningful experiences to unlock the language barrier of autism. This is what Temple Grandin is telling us to do.

16

PARENT POWER

How to Be a Proactive Parent

In this chapter I am going to empower you to be able to work effectively with your child. Whether your child is language delayed or at risk for ASD, the goals are the same: to stimulate your child's communication by following a developmental strategy. As we know, the number of children diagnosed with ASD has increased sharply. We also know that the earlier the intervention, the better the outcome. Unfortunately, valuable time passes by quickly while waiting for the evaluation process to begin. At its completion, parents must attend follow-up meetings, find therapists, and coordinate a therapy schedule. During this time many parents feel a sense of desperation. Some try to privately employ a speech and language clinician and ABA therapist. These specialists come with a large price tag, since services may be necessary every day. Parents hope that their personal health and medical insurance will pay in full, or in part, for these services, easing the financial burden. In many instances, insurance does not cover the service or will cover only a number of visits. As a result, it is obvious to me that you should be able to step up to the plate with confidence resulting in a sense of accomplishment. This part of the book is all about you, and how I can help you equip your home and implement strategies to help stimulate your child.

Working with your child will be challenging; however, knowing that you are being proactive, not wasting time, and following a strategy will eliminate feelings of being powerless. There are many productive ways to help your child both in and out of your home. Let's begin.

OBSERVING YOUR CHILD'S PEERS

Being a proactive parent means you are ready and willing to work with your child. You've already read about typical speech and language development. Now I want you to put this information into real time. The first thing to do is observe your child's typically developing peers. I want you to focus on what they are actually doing regarding their speech, language, and socialization development. This is an important first step. You may be randomly comparing the strengths of other children to the weaknesses of your child. I don't want you to take this negative approach. Your child has her own unique strengths; you just need to find them. By observing other children you will discover valuable information, as long as you go about it in the right way. Keep in mind that girls are usually stronger than boys in speech and language development. If your child is a twenty-four-month-old boy, focus on boys of the same age. There are many places where you can observe your child's peers: play dates, the park, birthday parties, Mommy and Me classes, even the waiting room in the pediatrician's office. Use the following chart to listen, observe, and record what you learn. Use your binder to set up a Speech, Language, Socialization Inventory Log, with the following information. You should try to make three to five separate observations. Make photocopies.

Speech, Language, Socialization Inventory Log

Date _____

Who is being observed (no names): [boy or girl] _____

Age in years and months _____

Place of observation/setting_____

Describe the setting_____

What are the children talking about? _____

How many words do they use? one word, two words, phrases, sentences?

_____

Write a short sample of what the child/children actually say. _____

Can you understand what the children are saying? _____

What are the children playing or doing? _____

How are they playing? _____

Are they playing with other children or by themselves? _____

Is their behavior cooperative or disruptive?_____

Will your child fit in? Explain. _____

What could you do to help your child fit in? _____

Is this a realistic goal to work on? _____

INCLUSION PLAY

By observing typically developing children, you may find opportunities where your child fits in and can be included. It is possible that you have not considered inclusion play because you think your child is too delayed. Or you may be embarrassed because your child is developing differently. Don't put blocks in your way. I want you to see that typically developing children also have a wide range of how and when they develop. You will learn that not all children talk while they play. Some like to play alone. Others may be more into hands-on play, like digging and building, while some children prefer to be mommy and daddy while talking and role-playing. Try to identify children who are a good fit to play with your child. This will give her early exposure to language and social skills with others. If appropriate, keep the possibility open for her to play with children who are a little younger. Remember, the literature points toward the belief that the earlier the child at risk for ASD is involved in intervention, the better the outcome. Play is an important intervention.

PRESCHOOL YEARS

Why am I asking you to make all these observations? Your child is probably between the ages of two and five years old and may benefit by attending a preschool program. If your child is high functioning she may thrive in an inclusion class. Inclusion, also referred to as mainstreaming or merging, is when children with special needs attend class with their typically developing peers. If your child is on the high level of the spectrum, she may benefit by being in an inclusive environment that offers exposure to positive role models, social development, and academics. Currently, high functioning children with ASD are successfully blending into mainstream education. Before making this decision, be sure that the curriculum is language enriched and that teachers and staff are prepared to help with behavior and socialization challenges.

Children with *serious* language and behavior disorders will require an intensive, one-to-one program focused on language stimulation and behavior management, led by well-trained professionals in autism. An inclusive setting will not meet their needs, nor would it be appropriate at this time.

In this chapter I discussed the importance of observing other children to find positive opportunities for play and socialization. Preschool programs are important, especially for children who need speech and language stimulation. For children who are on the higher end of the spectrum, an inclusion program may be the right placement. For children with serious language and behavior challenges, a more contained, special education program will be necessary. Regardless of whether your child attends a preschool program or not, having a well-designed language-enriched home environment is essential. In the next chapter I will talk to you about setting up your home.

⑰

SETTING UP THE HOME ENVIRONMENT

Your home is an important familiar place where your child can make many advances under your direction. In this chapter you will learn what a valuable resource your home can be.

THE HOME LEARNING CENTER

Early childhood classrooms traditionally have fun, well-organized, hands-on areas called learning centers. These centers stimulate natural creative play with a central theme. They are a place that is comfortable, enjoyable, and language enriched. I want you to create a type of learning center in your home. One of the most popular centers is probably the kitchen or home living center. Centers are designed with toys, pictures, books, games, or furnishings that relate to the theme. It is a place where children play, talk, and socialize. Children blossom in these settings as they explore and learn.

YOUR HOME PLAY-LEARNING CENTER

You are going to set up a play-learning space that replicates a learning center. It will serve two functions: to encourage meaningful play, language development, and socialization; and it will be a comforting place where your child can go by himself. The area should be quiet, free of distractions, and uncluttered. You don't need a whole room; in fact, using a room, den, or basement will be too large. You want to create a play-learning space, which has a warm, secure feeling. Once you find the right place, section off a corner approximately five feet by five feet with a room divider, screen, or other type of partition. Make sure there are no barriers blocking your view of your child. In one corner you will want to have a children's-size soft chair, or cushion with pillows, and a blanket to create a comforting place to rest. Also include a children's small table and chair. Lighting is important, so try to install a dimmer switch, which will allow you to adjust the light and create a tranquil atmosphere. If your child enjoys music, consider small speakers.

Do not use this space for time-out or punishment. This area should be a positive place where your child can thrive, by himself, with you, and, when ready, a friend. Look at the diagram to get an idea of how to design the space. The figure on the next page shows how to set up the home learning center area.

SAMPLE CENTER DIAGRAM

It is neither necessary nor suggested for you to make a permanent design in this space. You will want the ability to change themes and toys, to coincide with what your child needs to learn, and what she enjoys. If your child is hyperactive and easily distractible, you may want to set up a neutral space with limited stimulation. Over time, when your child's behavior improves, and for children who are not distractible, you will want to make the space more interesting. Using decorations to highlight the change of seasons, special times of the year, family photos, holidays both religious and civic, a birthday, or an upcoming family event will help your child learn about the world.

THEMES FOR YOUR HOME PLAY CENTER

Now that we have discussed the function of the play-learning space, here are some suggested themes you may want to consider. One last point: creative environments are important for both boys and girls. Make them fun and gender neutral. Don't limit your child's experiences because you believe they are only for boys or girls. Boys can cook and girls can build. Children learn and have a lot of fun with realistic play.

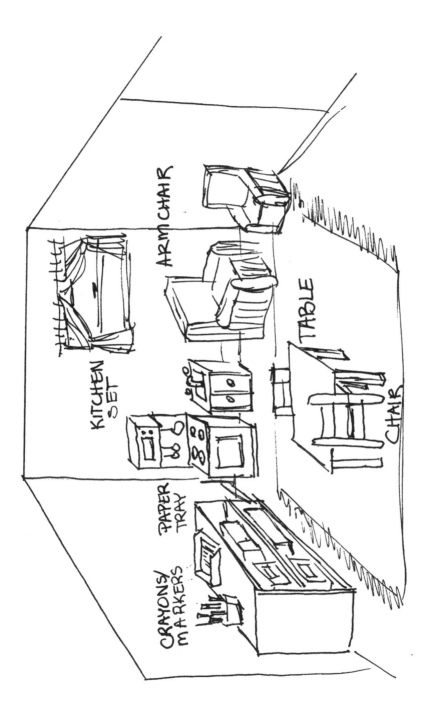

KITCHEN SET

ARM CHAIR

TABLE

CHAIR

PAPER TRAY

CRAYONS/ MARKERS

Play Themes

Kitchen/living room

Laundry and clothing: toy ironing board, iron, clothesline, clothespins, hangers

Animals: pets, farm animals, zoo animals, jungle animals, water animals, birds

Transportation: car, truck, plane, helicopter, train, space shuttle, boat, wagon

Blocks, balls, Legos, building toys

Puppets, dolls, people figures, carriage, toy high chair, toy crib, Sesame Street figures, Disney figures, popular cartoon figures . . . I do not recommend any superheroes or action figures known to be violent or aggressive. You do not want to encourage destructive play in any way.

Plants and fish: a grown plant, seeds that you plant with your child, a bowl with goldfish, an aquarium

Toy tools and work bench

Supermarket: toy cart, toy foods, fruits and vegetables

Music: toy instruments

Or choose your own theme!

Whatever theme you choose, you will need to collect appropriate toys, props, games, and pictures to make it a language enriched experience. You want your child to learn words for different objects and their functions, action words, and how to play in a meaningful way. You want her to pay attention and focus so she can transfer what she learns into her memory for later use.

It is important that the area be well organized. Too much clutter will be distracting. Keep toys in plastic baskets that have covers, or ziplock plastic bags, and label the contents. Realistic toys are the best. Besides the standard toy animals, people figures, toy tools, household appliances, and shopping props, consider a dress up area. Dressing up stimulates creativity, play acting, language, and socialization. Collect dress up props such as costumes, different occupational hats, toy money, a cash register, shopping bags, doctor's kit, glasses, and children's size sports equipment, to name a few. You can build or buy a doll's house and furnish the different rooms with toy furniture. When choosing toys, remember realistic toys are recommended. No guns, swords, violent objects, or scary action figures. You may have many realistic toys in your home; if not, you can make them out of boxes, cardboard, or for those who are handier, scrap wood. Be creative. If family or friends ask for suggestions for a holiday or birthday gift, give them a choice of some realistic toys that would benefit your child.

Besides having toys, you may want to start a small library. If your child has reached a stage where books are enjoyable I recommend nonfiction books, books that are true. Nonfiction books are preferable for two reasons: they help build vocabulary and knowledge, and they are realistic. Fantasy stories are too abstract and complex. Reading about a fairy, mermaid, or a train that talks is confusing and significantly counterproductive.

Scholastic has an excellent collection of nonfiction books for young children. Also, speak to the librarian at your local library. Librarians will be able to help you find nonfiction children's books on many subjects. If your child has an interest in trains, look for a book all about trains. You will find interesting information to expand your child's language and understanding. Later you can color, cut out, play with, or make trains. You can even take a ride on a train. Draw pretend tracks while saying, "choo-choo." Make your train move across the floor.

Choose books with pictures and few words. Encourage your child to point to different pictures, repeat words, and turn the pages. By using nonfiction books your child will build a useful vocabulary and collect facts. If books are not yet meaningful to your child, or she does not use them appropriately, wait for a later time.

18

HOW TOYS CONTRIBUTE TO LANGUAGE DEVELOPMENT

Many toys, when used appropriately, help stimulate speech, language, and social development. It's a good idea to buy a variety of toys within the same category such as animal or transportation toys. Your child will learn to analyze the characteristics that toys of the same category have in common. This expansion of ideas is important for language development and memory.

For example, let's pretend you buy your child a bag of ten plastic deep-sea toy fish. You look and talk about the different parts of the fish, fill a bowl with water and pretend that the fish are swimming. Together, look at picture books about fish. Then, take your child to the pet store, and be sure to bring her toy fish in a clear reclosable plastic bag. Look at the fish in the big aquarium. Look at the fish in the bag. "Fish!" you say, pointing to the fish in the tank. "Fish," you say, taking one of the fish out of the bag. Encourage your child to say or sign fish. This is the way to merge toys with language stimulation in a natural setting and expand learning beyond the home experience. Through this activity your child is developing more ideas about fish. Hopefully, your child will soon be ready to say *fish* when he sees one. This is a successful language experience using toys and the environment.

There are many categories of toys your child will enjoy playing with. You can collect toy animals such as pets, jungle, zoo, and farm animals. You can collect fruits, vegetables, dinosaurs, musical instruments, toy furniture, and toy dishes to set a table. Transportation toys such as cars, trucks, motorcycles, boats, planes, helicopters, and trains are also lots of fun. By adding props such as a toy bridge, tracks, a parking area, runway, or dock, the experience becomes more realistic and exciting. You will help your child expand her ideas, and learn more words. Having a variety of toys is beneficial because typically developing kids learn through play. Then a trip to an airport, dock, bridge, or train will naturally place ideas in context.

Play with one category of toys at a time. This will help your child create an image of what the toys have in common. For example, land transportation toys have wheels. They can go and stop. At the same time he will learn the names of the different toys and how they function in similar ways. Using random toys is not as productive. Also, don't mix different categories of toys together. You don't want a potpourri of cars, toy foods, and birds. Keep toys well organized. Have two categories of toys available in your child's play-learning center, accessible on a low shelf. You want her to be able to take a box and play independently. If she is playing in a meaningful way let her continue to explore and discover. If she is not, take away the box and focus on one toy. Talk about the name of the toy, its function, and show her how to play with it. Whether she is verbal or nonverbal, realistic toys, followed by natural experiences, are valuable and necessary to help stimulate speech, language, and socialization.

A last note about toys. Have you ever gone to someone's house and entered to find an obstacle course, cluttered with toys? This is what I call a balagan! Toys in the living room, kitchen, even toys stuck between the sofa cushions. This is exactly what you don't want: confusion and disorder. This isn't a positive environment for any child, especially your child. Do not allow this to happen.

BUILDING VOCABULARY BEYOND TOYS

You can expand the toy experience in many ways beyond toys to increase vocabulary. You can have your child play dress up, or dress up a doll while discussing different types of clothing, culminating with a visit to a shoe store or clothing store. Or you could work on naming different kinds of clothing as well as towels, sheets, and pillowcases, culminating with doing the laundry. The supermarket is a great place to discuss lots of different categories, such as fruits, vegetables, meat, drinks, cookies, ice cream; things in boxes, cans, bottles, or cartons; things that are cold; things that are frozen; things you drink; things you eat. You could look for foods that are round, green, or red; foods that have leaves; sliced breads, rolls, buns for hot dogs, buns for hamburgers, muffins, challah; different shapes of pasta—spaghetti, linguini, elbows, shells, rigatoni; things made of paper—toilet paper, napkins, paper towels; and different types of soap. How about products made specifically for children? Find the diapers, shampoo, cereal, sunscreen, vitamins, Band-Aids, and toothpaste all packaged in fun, creative ways for kids. Take one off the shelf and talk about it. Look at the different logos on Band-Aids for kids—Sponge Bob, Elmo. Supermarkets also have pet food, baby food, snacks, and candy. For a child, there is a university of knowledge up and down the aisles. Keep a log of new vocabulary words your child learns and uses. The chart below shows how to keep a log for new words. Make photocopies and add to your binder.

In this chapter we talked about the ways toys may be used to help stimulate speech and language development. It is important to use realistic toys and engage in realistic play. Children at risk for ASD do not know the name and function of the objects around them. Using realistic toys will help to bring meaning to their confused lives. Keeping toys organized and in categories will also help to build understanding. Talk about the names of the toys you are using and how you are playing with them. Remember that playing with random toys without a purpose is not productive. You should be focused on the goal of making experiences meaningful. Also, choose nonfiction books. Fantasy material is not meaningful. As a culminating activity visit different places so your child can experience language in a natural setting.

In the next chapter I am going to talk about designing different themes in your child's play-learning space.

Log for New Words			
Date	New word	Where were you?	What were you doing that prompted the word?

HOW TO DESIGN AND USE YOUR HOME PLAY-LEARNING CENTER

We have talked about how children learn through experience. In this chapter I am going to show you how to design a home learning center so your child has the opportunity to be immersed in a meaningful learning environment during most of her waking hours. Here are some suggestions.

The kitchen learning center is probably the most popular environment for children to play in. Here is an example of how to design a kitchen center experience. You will need a toy kitchen. If you don't have a toy kitchen you can use cartons from the supermarket to design a stove, sink, and refrigerator. With a little creativity, colored markers, or the help of an artistic friend you can construct an effective kitchen. You do not have to spend money on expensive toys. Put toy pots, pans, and an oven mitt in a basket. Place make-believe food on the table, in a cabinet, or the refrigerator. In another basket have toy dishes, cups, forks, knives, spoons, and napkins.

The goal is to have your child learn through experience, build her vocabulary, and increase language use through appropriate play in the kitchen. Talk to your child while you guide her. Tell her the names of the objects as she uses them. Ask questions, "What are you doing?" "Oh, you're cooking!" "What are you making?" "What can I do?" "Show me your favorite food." "Put the hot dog on the plate." Tell her the action words as she is mixing, pouring, cutting, rolling. You can use play dough to demonstrate rolling, cutting, pressing, and twisting. You can make foods out of different colored play dough. Use cookie cutters to make different shapes. Some cookie cutters come in shapes for different themes. For example, for Thanksgiving Day there may be cookie cutters shaped like a turkey, a pumpkin, a little boy or girl Pilgrim, the Mayflower, or a Native American.

For children who are verbal, play a food lotto game. Put matching pictures of foods on index cards and play a matching game. Matching is a visual, hands-on activity that can help with vocabulary and building concepts. For example, after your child is able to match the two apple cards together you can tell her that an apple is a fruit, it grows on trees, and we eat them in apple sauce and apple pie. In addition, through matching, children learn concepts of same and different, which are important early childhood skills. If your child is higher functioning, play a concentration game with the cards. Start by placing six matching cards face down on a children's table. Your child will turn the cards over one at a time to match a pair. This type of game helps with focus, attention, and memory, all important skills for learning.

How will I know if my child is having a positive, meaningful experience in the play kitchen? First, give your child some time to explore and discover on his own. For this to be a meaningful experience, he needs to pretend to cook. He should use pots and pans by the stove, and the toy foods to cook. He should try to set the table. If there is a toy juice or milk container, eggs, or cheese, he should put the foods into the refrigerator. He should use the oven mitt when using the oven. To promote socialization, encourage him to sit at the table. Have a snack and drink ready to make the experience more realistic. The snack belongs on the plate. Help him pour a drink into the cup. You may want to have a doll at the table. Encourage your child to feed the doll.

What can I expect if my child is not having a meaningful experience? If your child is not having a meaningful experience, this is what may happen. While your child is exploring the kitchen center, instead of appropriate play he throws the food, dumps the basket of pots and pans on the floor, and taps the toy knife repeatedly on the table. When you take the knife away, he throws a tantrum and kicks the table. This reaction is expected for children who do not have meaningful ideas. If your child behaves like this, for now, he is lost in his world. He just does not understand the experience, or how to act. He does not know what the objects are, or how to use them. He is at a low level of functioning, with a significant block in language development and communication. He is understandably frustrated and very upset. What can you learn from this experience? How do you move forward?

TURNING A NEGATIVE EXPERIENCE
INTO A LEARNING EXPERIENCE

Although upsetting, you can definitely learn and move forward from this experience by analyzing what happened and redirecting your child's behavior for the future. It is apparent that he needs to become familiar and comfortable with his environment, both inside and outside. To understand his point of view better, imagine the following. You are on a camping trip and start to explore the woods around you. Before you realize it, you are lost. Everything looks the same, you have no clear landmark to regain your bearings, and it's starting to get dark. Many adults would panic. Think of your child as lost. As an adult you can call someone's name for help or look up to the sky for direction. Anticipating problems that could occur on a camping trip, you probably took your cell phone and had a compass in your pocket. Your child is helpless. He is lost, scared, and without any survival options. The difference is, he is not in the woods; he is in your home. He throws or kicks everything because everything is the same. He does not understand their names or differences, what things are or how to use them. Tantrums are the only way he can call for help. To harness destructive and distractive behavior, you will work to give his environment meaning. You can begin by making him more aware of his surroundings. This would include learning about the rooms of the house and other places that are part of your routine. You need to help him discover and learn about his confusing, scary world.

In this chapter I talked about how to set up a learning center in your home to help stimulate speech language and socialization. Your child can make many discoveries in a home learning center. Playing appropriately and meaningfully is the most important goal. Based upon your child's level of functioning you can increase the challenge by playing picture and matching games. However, you may find that your child is just not ready for a complex experience. He throws tantrums and reacts destructively. You need to try to put yourself in your child's shoes and understand how lost he is in his world. By simplifying experiences you will help him learn about the world around him, gain meaning, and reduce counterproductive behavior.

In the next chapter I will talk about the supplies you will need to help your child learn creatively without toys.

SUPPLIES

There are many imaginative and inventive experiences children have without toys. In this chapter I am going to tell you what you need for your child to discover his own creativity.

Imagine a baseball player without a bat or a chef without a spoon; it just would not work. The same is true for children. Children need children's equipment. To start off, you should have a child's table and chair set up in their play-learning center. Sitting at a table is a big accomplishment for many children. It's a step toward self-control. Even if it's only for seconds, with time and positive reinforcement she will be able to sit longer and longer. Next, she needs children's supplies. Second to toys, kids need crayons, markers, pencils, water paint, a glue stick, tape, and scissors. They need paper, lined, unlined, colored, and graph, available in trays that can be easily reached. Buy stickers and precut shapes for gluing. Soon she will discover all the fun, hands-on things she can do by herself. Find opportunities for her to make her own cards. Keep blank envelopes and plain folded paper in a box to design birthday and holiday wishes. Let her put on the stamp and drop it in the mailbox. Doodling and scribbling is all part of discovery. In addition keep some picture books, connect-the-dots books, and coloring books on hand. There are nonfiction coloring books that she can learn from, such as coloring books about animals, places, community workers, plants and trees, foods, transportation, and sports, to name a few. You may find that she will want to sit at the table, look at the pictures, and turn the pages. This will really be a sign of improved attention and focus.

Have these supplies out, organized, and ready for your child to use independently. Just as grown-ups enjoy their living room to unwind, read, or watch television, your child's play area should be a place that offers her the same luxury. In fact, when she's there, put out a juice box and a few pretzels!

In this chapter you read about "kid" supplies and how important it is to have them easily accessible. Coloring, scribbling, and play writing are activities your child can do independently. It is a fun way to foster positive learning skills, such as focus and attention. If you are concerned about markers dropping and paint spilling, you can protect the flood with a plastic mat. Cleaning up is also a learning experience, so have sponges and paper towels available as well. Give your child the responsibility to clean up.

Now that you have set up an area for your child with center themes, toys, and supplies, it will be important for you to establish your child's baseline for communication and play. Does your child use words? How many? Are they appropriate? Does your child play meaningfully? Does he throw toys? Recording developmental information about your child allows you to measure progress, observe what your child likes, and learn which situations trigger destructive behavior. In the next chapter, I am going to explain why accountability is important, especially for a language delayed child or a child at risk.

21

ACCOUNTABILITY

If your child is delayed the probability of needing special education services is highly likely. You have read about the broad spectrum of behaviors and abilities children at risk demonstrate. Having your child in the right program will be very important. How will you be able to advocate for your child? How will you be able to credibly report your child's strengths and weaknesses? The answer is accountability, and that's what this chapter is about.

You are now prepared with hands-on experiences, toys, and supplies. Working with your child will be a continuous work in progress. Accountability will be as important as the time you spend with her. It will be significantly valuable because it will allow you to look back over a period of time and assess progress, identify your child's strengths and weaknesses, advocate for your child when it comes to school placement and therapy, and share information with the speech therapist and other related professionals.

Testing and evaluations will be another part of your child's school experience. Usually, evaluations take place over one or two days. Often the evaluator is meeting your child for the first time and does not know her at the time of testing. Decisions are being made based upon observations and her performance. Your child may not be doing her best at the time. She could be distracted, having difficulty adjusting to a new person, or upset by noises or light in the room. It is possible that the evaluator may determine that your child is functioning at a lower level, lower than her capability. You try to explain that it's a bad day or the chemistry is not right. Although true, parents are often seen as defensive or in denial, seeing their child through a biased view. You don't want that to happen to you, and it won't if you are accountable. It is in your best interest and the best interest of your child to record what you are doing and what you have observed. Documentation will be the best way to present your child's strengths and weaknesses, and the best way to obtain services she needs. Document your child's progress. Copy the log sheet to help you track progress.

Keep the log sheets organized in your binder.

As you read, this chapter stresses the importance of record keeping. We keep records all the time: dates of immunizations, the day of baby's first step, when to give the next dose of medicine. It is especially important to keep records regarding your child's communication development. It will allow you to be her best advocate. It is understandable that even though you want to do what is best for your child, the stress can be exhausting.

In the next chapter, I want to talk about you, the parent, and how to prepare for the challenges ahead.

LOG SHEET	
Date	Describe Progress

22

PERSONALLY PREPARING
FOR THE CHALLENGE

If your child is language delayed, he may require special education services during the early childhood years, and possibly during the beginning elementary grades. If your child is diagnosed on the autism spectrum, special services may be necessary throughout his education. In this chapter I am going to talk about preparing for the challenge.

Understand that at times, working with your language delayed child will cause frustration and present obstacles. If he is nonverbal it may take time for him to say words. If you feel your tolerance is "waning" take a break. If saying words is too difficult or he is just not ready, you may need to decide to implement nonverbal strategies, something you may not have wanted to do. If he has temper tantrums, engages in destructive or self-injurious behavior, or cannot focus productively, you need to consult with a certified ABA specialist or a psychologist who specializes in behavior modification therapy. These professionals are all an essential part of an intervention team. Accept their help. Not only do they know how to help with behavior management, they also know how to help with important quality of life issues, especially if you have other children. To help you along, I've created the ten-step preparation program. Think of it as a warm-up before you begin working with your child.

THE TEN-STEP PREP

1. Make uninterrupted time available in ten- to twenty-minute intervals—no cell phones.
2. Realize your child does not comprehend the world around him.
3. He does not know the names or functions of objects, people, or actions.
4. Although he can hear, he may not understand what he hears.
5. Speak in a calm, conversational tone that can be heard.
6. Choose an environment that is quiet, with limited distractions.
7. Make sure he makes eye contact with you or the object you are using; visual prompts are necessary.
8. Speak slowly.
9. Use few words.
10. Establish a reward system. You know what your child likes and is willing to work for. Associate rewards with positive behavior.

With all the focus on your child, it is time to focus on you. Having and maintaining the right emotional well-being is essential. Your child needs you to succeed. This requires a healthy parent. Meditation is one way to establish a sense of calm in light of stress. Try this meditation.

PARENT MEDITATION

Fill in your child's name:

"_____ may not understand what I'm saying. My words may be like a foreign language, a language she does not use or comprehend. I will speak slowly with few words. I will use visual examples, pictures, toys, hands-on experiences, signs, and gestures to help her gain knowledge about the world around her. She is frustrated, confused, and maybe even scared. I will be mindful of her limitations, yet prepared to be her advocate."

Along with this meditation try five to ten minutes of deep breathing exercises or a yoga routine. You may want to meditate and practice a relaxation exercise two to three times a day. Your goal is to achieve a sense of calm and relaxation.

PART TWO SUMMARY

Working with your child will be challenging; however, there are many things you can do to be proactive. Creating a stimulating language-based learning atmosphere in your home is important. Arranging a comfortable, secure, private space will hopefully be a place that your child will enjoy. Having realistic toys and kid's supplies encourages independent play and productive use of time. Without overstimulating your child, be sure that you offer visual experiences. At the beginning, especially if your child is nonverbal, the use of pictures and objects will help her understand the world around her. I have known many parents who have felt helpless and frustrated watching their language delayed child spend endless hours playing with the same toy or watching the same video or DVD. Now empowered with hands-on activities and a developmental plan, your practical efforts will replace feelings of powerlessness.

In part three, I will give you the tools to become your child's paraspeech partner. From producing sounds, to words, I will present you with twenty-seven different categories totaling more than seven hundred words that children should know. We will begin with single words. Through repetition, visual experiences, and frequency you will work to help your child break through the barrier of autism.

Part Three

SOUNDS TO WORDS

TECHNIQUES TO STIMULATE SPEECH, LANGUAGE, AND SOCIALIZATION

INTRODUCTION

Part three is all about stimulating communication. It's about the nonverbal child who needs to discover his voice, the child who needs to employ gestures and signs as a means of expression, and ultimately, the child who can achieve verbal competence. Next, I focus on the single utterance by presenting twenty-seven different categories totaling more than seven hundred basic words children should know. Based upon your child's ability and willingness to speak, she will either use words or signs. In fact, you may decide that combining the sign with the word may be the best technique for your child. Now I will introduce the nonverbal child.

23

HELPING YOUR NONVERBAL CHILD

In this chapter I will talk about the importance of exhaled air and making sounds. This will be important if your child is not making sounds, making few sounds, or cannot blow out a stream of air.

Some children never experienced a period of babbling, or it started and stopped suddenly. Some children make a few single sounds. Although these sounds do not appear to have meaning, they are significant. Your child is showing a willingness to vocalize. Consider sounds as her attempt to communicate. In time, you may realize that the sounds have a purpose. More importantly, making sounds may be a first step toward using speech.

ACTIVITY 1: PRODUCING EXHALED AIR

Pretend you are blowing up a balloon. The air that you are blowing through your mouth is called exhaled air. The air you breathe in is called inhaled air. We use exhaled air to speak. To know if your child can produce a strong flow of exhaled air, have him blow bubbles out of a bubble wand. Some children can't do this for the following reasons: they may not know what to do; the exhaled stream of air may be weak, too short, or spitty.

Having a strong breathing pattern for inhaling and exhaling air is necessary for speech production. Strong breathing is also important in order to project your voice to be heard by others. You want your child not only to speak but also to be heard. If your child is nonverbal, uses few sounds, or cannot be heard, strengthening exhaled air flow is important.

Warning: Do not let your child play with balloons. They can get caught in the back of the throat covering the entrance to the trachea (air supply). As a result, balloons have been known to cause choking and even death. Do not use candles.

ACTIVITY 2: MAKING SOUNDS

At the same time you are working on producing exhaled air, begin to work on stimulating sounds. Face your child and encourage eye contact. You want her to see your facial expression, lips, and eyes. The area should be free of distractions and noise. Make the experience enjoyable. Have juice or a lollypop available. Reward by giving her a "sip or a lick!"

Ways to Stimulate Sounds

Humming: Become familiar with nursery rhymes, children's songs, or favorite family melodies. Hum these songs to her while making eye contact. Many nursery rhymes and children's songs have catchy beats, melodies, and different vocal tones. You can try clapping hands to the beat. Hopefully this will be a pleasurable, socially engaging experience. Reward any attempt she makes to vocalize. Hum songs during the day. You want her to become familiar with the tunes. Begin humming a few notes; encourage her to continue.

Babbling: Your child may not have gone through the "babbling" stage of communication development. Or it is possible that she started babbling and then for no apparent reason stopped. Babbling is when children play with the use of different sounds. Making sounds and hearing sounds is usually enjoyable. Children continue this vocal play as they start to develop speech. While children are babbling, parents babble back. There is a lot of eye contact, smiling, and social interaction. Encourage and reward any attempt she makes to produce sounds. Try to encourage babbling by saying silly repetitive sounds. Make sure you are looking at your child and encourage her to look at you. Example: ma-ma-ma-ma-ma-ma-ma, b-b-b-b-b-b-b-b, p-p-p-p-p-p-p-p.

Music: Use musical instruments to encourage sound production. The following musical toys are fun and easy for you and your child to use:

- Xylophone
- Drum
- Tambourine
- Shaker toy
- Rattle
- Bell
- Triangle
- Children's keyboard

Keep a variety of toy musical instruments in a plastic box or container and label: Musical Instruments to Stimulate Sounds. Be sure to have a picture of a musical instrument on the container so your child can identify what's inside on her own. Choose one of the instruments and show your child how to use it. While playing, use different sounds, sing to the beat. You can clap and dance as long as it is not too stimulating. Sing la-la-la-la. Have your child choose an instrument and help her use it. Continue to sing sounds to the beat. Encourage her to sing. Tap your finger by her lips or chin for sensory reinforcement. Make the sounds slowly and make sure she watches your lips. Try different instruments and different sounds. If she makes sounds, reward her. Encourage her to keep trying.

Important note: No matter what activity you are working on, you want the experience to be meaningful. To do this, I would like you to answer the following three questions. Does your child

Use the instruments appropriately?
Know how to shake the bells?
Use the stick appropriately to play the xylophone, or drums?

If you answer yes, that means she is using the toy instruments in meaningful ways. It shows she has appropriate ideas and an understanding about their use. This is an important and positive observation; record this information on the Log Sheet in your binder.

However, if she is throwing the toys or tapping the drumstick over and over, her behavior is neither purposeful nor appropriate. For now, she does not have meaningful ideas about the instruments, nor does she know how to use them. Although you are using the instruments to stimulate sounds, you will need to show her how to play with them. When she knows how to play with the instruments appropriately, she will have gained understanding about their use.

As she acquires more knowledge, the next step will be for her to associate the toy with its name. Remember, using objects or toys without meaning or understanding does not enforce language development. Meaning is necessary for cognitive development and breaking through the language barrier.

In this chapter, I explained the importance of strengthening exhaled air to produce sounds. In the next chapter, I am going to show you how to encourage communication using nonverbal language.

(24)

NONVERBAL LANGUAGE

A lot can be communicated using nonverbal language. You can let some-one know if you are happy, sad, tired, or even sick. In this chapter, I am going to show you how you can encourage communication and socialization using nonverbal language. If your child has a willingness to use nonverbal language, you will have made a big breakthrough in communication.

Typically developing children express themselves quite successfully by using nonverbal language. Right now, if your child is not making sounds, using words, or making sounds that are intelligible, employing nonverbal communication techniques is important and essential. Waiting for speech to develop, or be understandable, may cost valuable time. Using alterna-tive methods may help your child develop language, gain knowledge, and understand the world around her, which is clearly your goal. I have made a list of fifty important nonverbal gestures that have meaning. When used purposefully and appropriately, these actions may be the beginning of com-munication and socialization for your child.

FIFTY MEANINGFUL NONVERBAL ACTIONS

You want to encourage communication and socialization even if your child is not using or cannot use speech. Use the following gestures regularly with him whenever appropriate, and encourage him to participate. If he needs help, hold his hand and model the gesture as you say the word. To make the gestures more realistic and to help with understanding, use props. For example, if you are acting out digging, use a shovel. Gestures are visual, hands-on, and helpful for your child. Make picture cards by laminating the pictures on index cards with clear wrapping tape; they will not tear and will last longer. Paste an ice cream stick on the back so you can hold it like a sign. Show your child different pictures. See if he can act out what he sees. Later on show him a picture and see if he knows the word. For example, show him the picture of clapping. Can he copy what he sees and clap? Can he look at the picture and say clap? These are your goals. Keep the pictures in a plastic reclosable bag. Practice often.

Practice the fifty gestures on the next page with your child. Copy the list and place it in your binder. Indicate the date he uses them appropriately and independently.

MEANINGFUL NONVERBAL ACTIONS

1. waving hi or bye-bye
2. clapping
3. hugging
4. pointing
5. throwing a kiss
6. combing hair
7. brushing teeth
8. cutting with scissors
9. washing hair
10. eating
11. drinking
12. throwing a ball
13. sweeping
14. swimming
15. bowling
16. playing tennis
17. playing golf
18. flying like a bird or plane
19. blowing out candles
20. watering a plant or flowers
21. dancing
22. kicking a ball
23. driving
24. washing hands
25. pouring
26. turning a page
27. reading a book
28. pushing a shopping cart/carriage
29. skating
30. opening a door
31. rowing a boat
32. pushing
33. pulling
34. climbing
35. swinging
36. opening a jar
37. putting on shoes
38. buttoning
39. putting on gloves
40. mixing cake batter
41. chewing
42. painting
43. hopping
44. jumping
45. eating a lollipop
46. fishing
47. peeling a banana
48. digging
49. zipping up/down
50. batting a baseball

In this chapter, you have learned that children can communicate many ideas using nonverbal actions. However, these gestures are random actions to describe an idea. There is often a need to substitute informal gestures with a formal nonverbal language system, understood by others, employing the use of signs. In the next chapter, I am going to talk about two formal nonverbal languages, American Sign Language (ASL) and Signed English (SE).

㉕

SIGNING

Some children remain nonverbal while others are unable to articulate intelligible speech. In these circumstances, the need for an alternative language system that is widely used and understood by others is required. The two nonverbal languages widely used in the United States are American Sign Language and Signed English.

Signing is different from gestures. Gestures are informal actions. You can make up your own effective gestures for words or ideas, as long as the person you are going to use them with knows what they mean. You may decide that a clap has one meaning and a snap another. People will not understand your gesture unless you tell them.

American Sign Language (ASL) and Signed English (SE) are different. They are both formal nonverbal languages widely understood. The significant difference is that ASL is not grammatically correct, Signed English is. By using ASL or Signed English you are using hand signs that are understood by millions of people. They are both languages like English. You cannot use any hand sign to be understood; you need to use the signs that represent the message you are trying to convey.

Some parents are reluctant to use signs with their child. They are afraid that signing will discourage verbal communication, and signing has limitations of being understood by others. As a result, parents often try signing as a last resort. Last resort means important time wasted.

If you are concerned about using sign language, combine signs with words. If the combination prompts your child to use words, then it was successful. If signing emerges as the exclusive way your child will communicate, then you've broken through the language barrier. All and all, signing is a valuable way for your child to build her vocabulary and promote communication. For some children the visual focus on the hand signs helps to stimulate communication. Signing has been used to stimulate speech and language with typically developing children specifically because of the visual cues. Try signing if your child is either nonverbal or hard to be understood. Keep in mind, without a way for your child to communicate, behavioral outbursts may be the result of serious frustration.

In this chapter, I have discussed the use of sign language. Some parents agree to use signs as a last resort because they are afraid that their children will not develop speech or will not be understood by others. Although it is understandable to have these feelings, the main goal is to offer your child an opportunity and a way to develop language and communicate. Remaining nonverbal may be part of her global disability, or her speech may be so unintelligible that relying on oral communication may be counterproductive. Regardless, signing offers a chance to promote communication and socialization. It may be the opportunity your child needs to learn how to express his overwhelming frustration and understand the world around him. Together with your child, you can learn to sign. At the end of this book you will find a list of websites where you can learn sign language. In the next chapter, I am going to talk to you about stimulating speech.

SEVENTY IMPORTANT SIGNS USING
AMERICAN SIGN LANGUAGE

Practice these seventy signs with your child. Photocopy and place in your binder. Record the date he uses them appropriately and independently.

yes	good	hot dog
no	point	chips
eating	give	ice cream
drinking	take	running
hungry	rain	jumping
thirsty	snow	kicking
toilet/bathroom	dress	walking
sit	bed	dancing
want	underwear	cooking
cookie	socks	washing
apple	pants/skirt	pouring
juice	shoes	mixing
water	coat	looking
go	hat	in
stop	book	out
come	ball	on
sleepy	dog	off
table	cat	up
chair	bird	down
mommy	fish	open
daddy	pizza	close
more	burger	big
thank you	milk	little
please		

26

STIMULATING
SPEECH SOUNDS

The ultimate goal is for your child to use speech to communicate. Finding that your child is willing and able to use words is a big developmental step. In this chapter, I will talk about childhood apraxia of speech, a neurological disorder that interferes with the ability to produce intelligible speech. I will provide you with a list of the speech sounds we use in English and when to expect these sounds to develop. I am including a speech sound checklist for you to record your child's speech sound development. First, I want to talk about the child who may be willing to use speech but cannot be understood.

CHILDHOOD APRAXIA OF SPEECH

Some children on the spectrum are nonverbal or use a few limited sounds. Others make and use sounds, but they cannot form the different sounds precisely enough to be understood. These children are seriously speech impaired. The diagnosis, childhood apraxia of speech (CAS), is a neurologically based disorder. Children with CAS have severe difficulty recognizing sound patterns and difficulty articulating a sequence of sounds to form words. CAS is the result of a problem in motor and sound planning. The muscles of the mouth and tongue are unable to move smoothly from sound to sound to produce clear speech. In addition, auditory processing confusion interferes with the ability to correctly identify speech sounds and the pattern of the sounds that are heard. To produce clear speech the brain needs to

- Recognize the pattern or order of the sounds in a word (e.g., basket not baksit)
- Accurately process the sound (e.g., cap not cab)
- Automatically stimulate the muscles responsible for speech

Low or weak muscle tone may cause poor or slow movement. In addition, muscles control the movement of the tongue, lips, soft palate, jaw, and cheeks. To work efficiently, they need to be strong and well toned, just like the muscles in other parts of the body. In addition, the neurological pathway must work efficiently.

Talk to the speech therapist if you have any concern about CAS. There are motor exercises, programs, and stimulation tools that may be helpful. Talk Tools is a company that specializes in oral-motor exercises and toys to help stimulate the mouth, lips, palate, and cheeks. You can contact them at www.talktools.com and request a catalog.

ENGLISH SPEECH SOUND CHECKLIST

Copy this list and place in your binder. Put a check mark next to the sounds your child can make.

Vowel Sounds

/a/	as in apple	/u/	as in uniform
/e/	as in egg	/oi/, /oy/	as in toy
/i/	as in igloo	/ow/	as in cow
/o/	as in octopus	/aw/	as in law
/u/	as in umbrella	/oo/	as in too
/a/	as in apron	/oo/	as in book
/e/	as in eagle	/y/	as in yo-yo
/i/	as in ice	/y/	as in daisy
/o/	as in open	/y/	as in fly
		/ir/	as in bird
		/er/	as in worker

The following chart gives you a range of when consonant sounds are expected to emerge.

Expected Age of Consonant Sounds

(Sander 1972)

/b/	as in bat	1.5 to 4.0 years of age
/d/	as in dog	2.0 to 4.0 years of age
/f/	as in farm	2.3 to 4.0 years of age
/g/	as in girl	2.0 to 4.0 years of age
/h/	as in hat	1.5 to 3.0 years of age
/j/	as in jump or giant	4.0 to 7.0 years of age
/k/	as in key or cat	2.0 to 4.0 years of age
/l/	as in lap	3.0 to 6.0 years of age
/m/	as in moon	1.5 to 3.0 years of age
/n/	as in now	1.5 to 3.0 years of age
/p/	as in pen	1.5 to 3.0 years of age
/q/	as in queen; this sound is a combination of /kw/	
/r/	as in red	3.0 to 6.0 years of age
/s/	as in sun or circle	3.0 to 8.0 years of age
/t/	as in tap	2.0 to 6.0 years of age
/v/	as in van	4.0 to 8.0 years of age
/w/	as in we 1.5 to 3.0 years of age	
/x/	as in x-ray; this sound is a combination of /eks/	
/z/	as in zoo or xylophone	3.3 to 8.0 years of age
/sh/	as in shoe	3.3 to 7.0 years of age
/ch/	as in chair	3.3 to 7.0 years of age
/th/	as in the 4.3 to 8.0 years of age	
	as in thumb	4.3 to 7.0 years of age

CONDUCTING A SOUND INVENTORY

The success of this inventory will be based on your child's willingness to model the sounds you say, and your ability to identify the sounds that she makes. If your child is only making a few sounds, check off the sounds you can identify on your sound inventory checklist. If your child is willing to cooperate, ask her to repeat the individual sound or the sample word. Check off the sounds she can produce. You do not have to complete this inventory at one time. In fact, it is a good idea to vary the settings, such as a playground, park, gym, party, or pizza shop. You may get a better sample of sounds.

If your child is verbal, write down five to seven words she says. For example, if she says the word *bat* clearly, you know she can make the /b/ /a/ /t/ sounds. If she can only say /ba/, she is dropping the final /t/ sound. If you notice she is consistently dropping sound endings, that could be a goal to work on. Make different lists of one-syllable words with a consonant-vowel-consonant arrangement. Label the lists: final *b*, final *d*, final *g*, final *t*, final *p*. Under each heading write ten words that end in the target letter. *Example:* for final *t*: bat, mat, cat, hat, boat, coat, pet, pot, mitt, gate. Use pictures, real objects, or toys, and ask her to name or repeat the words, stressing the final consonant.

If she cannot produce a sound, for example /sh/, check to see if she is developmentally within the expected age range for onset. The expected onset for /sh/ is 3.3 to 7 years of age. If your child is within that age range, it is appropriate to work on the sound. Listen for more words and sound samples of her speech. Can she make the /s/ sound? It is possible that she can say the /s/ in sun but not in rice. In this situation, she can produce the sound but not at the end of a word. Make a list of words ending in the /s/ sound, such as house, bus, goose. Again, use visual aids along with the words.

In this chapter, I discussed the different sounds in English and the typical age of consonant sound onset. I have provided you with an organized checklist to record the sounds your child uses. I have also given you strategies on how to stimulate sounds. In the next chapter, I am going to address the nonverbal child and how to approach speech stimulation along with sound variety.

SOUNDS THAT
HAVE MEANING

What do I mean by sounds that have meaning, and why am I dedicating a chapter to it? Working with language delayed children, especially children at risk, requires you to be concrete while providing meaningful experiences. Random sounds have no meaning; nor are they concrete. If anything, they are meaningless and confusing and not what you want to present to a language delayed child. So how can you start to stimulate your child's speech in a simple way that is purposeful? In this chapter, I am going to show you how. In fact, I begin therapy with speech impaired typical children using the exact technique.

A good way to stimulate speech is by using simple, repetitive words or sounds. This sound list is concrete and meaningful. It is fun, simple, and an effective way to begin to introduce speech.

You will need small transportation toys, small people figures (mommy and daddy), and animal figures. You may also want to use colorful pictures and hands-on experiences.

Example: 1. beep-beep: car

The first repetitive sound is beep-beep. When associated with a land vehicle it has meaning.

Materials: a toy car or any land transportation vehicle.

Procedure: While playing with your child you will push the car and simultaneously say, "beep-beep, beep-beep."

Later on, to enhance comprehension you can ask your child: "What sound does the car make? Beep-beep!"

Goal: Continue until your child is able to use the car and independently say, "beep-beep."

Can your child answer the question: "What sound does the car make?" If she says, "beep-beep," that means that she understood your question, which is a very positive sign.

Use other land transportation toys.

Your child needs to expand "beep-beep" to the other toys as well (e.g., truck, bus).

You want your child to associate the sound beep-beep with the object.

If your child has a bicycle, take her for a ride and say beep-beep when someone or something is in her way.

You will continue this technique with the other repetitive sounds and associate them by matching the sound with the object. Record the date you practice and the date your child masters the goal.

Twenty-Five Simple Repetitive
Sounds Your Child Should Know

1. beep-beep: car
2. zoom-zoom: car/truck/ motorcycle
3. swish-swish: windshield wipers
4. toot-toot: boat
5. choo-choo: train
6. moo-moo: cow
7. oink-oink: pig
8. ney-ney: horse
9. baa-baa: sheep
10. cluck-cluck: chicken
11. ruff-ruff: dog
12. meow-meow: cat
13. quack-quack: duck
14. hoot-hoot: owl
15. da-da: daddy
16. ma-ma: mommy
17. tick-tick/tick-tock: clock
18. boom-boom/tap-tap: drum
19. knock-knock: door
20. clap-clap: hands
21. hi/bye-bye: waving
22. yum-yum: food
23. boo-boo: scratch or cut
24. la-la: singing
25. snip-snip: scissors/cutting

In this chapter, I discussed how to introduce simple repetitive sounds that are concrete and associated with meaning. Associating these meaningful sounds with meaningful actions will not only be a significant speech milestone, but a significant language milestone as well. From this point on, I am going to provide you with twenty-seven different categories totaling over seven hundred important words for children to know. Take your time and be patient. Until your child breaks the speech and language barrier, this will be a work in progress. Remember, repetition is essential.

㉘

STIMULATING A SINGLE
WORD VOCABULARY

In this chapter, you are going to find more than seven hundred single words divided into twenty-seven categories. Copy each of the category lists and put them in your binder to assess your child's progress and provide accountability. Follow the directions. Use the checklists to record the date you practice and the date your child has mastered the word. Some words may be too abstract or not relevant. You may want to consider them at a later time. You may find that important words are missing from the lists; please feel free to add them.

Your child is discovering a world he does not yet understand. You are going to bring meaning and knowledge to him by giving things names and functions. He will need to associate the word you say with the object or action, store the information in his memory, and learn to use the word meaningfully. Your goal is to help your child break through the language barrier. Be concrete, use pictures, objects, and visual experiences, and always make the time you spend with your child meaningful. Let's begin.

Category 1: Twenty-Five First Toy Words—Activity

Objective: To help your child identify twenty-five words for toys
Method (e.g., the word *ball*):

1. Present a ball to your child.
2. Say, "ball," "ball."
3. Reinforce: say, "ball."
4. Demonstrate: roll, bounce, toss the ball while saying "ball."
5. Repetition: say, "ball"; continue to act out its function.
6. If necessary introduce the sign for ball.

Steps toward understanding the word ball *in context.*
Directions: Show your child how to

1. Point to the ball.
2. Take the ball.
3. Give the ball.
4. Sign or say "ball."

After your child has achieved mastery you will tell your child:

1. Point to the ball.
2. Take the ball.
3. Give the ball.
4. Sign or say ball.

After achieving mastery you will ask your child:

1. "What is this?"
2. He will sign or say, "ball."

Continue this format for the remaining twenty-four toy words. Remember to record the practice dates and the date of mastery of the word.

Category 1: Twenty-Five First Toy Words Your Child Should Know

1. ball
2. doll
3. rattle
4. truck
5. car
6. motorcycle
7. bus
8. plane
9. helicopter
10. bike
11. train
12. teddy bear
13. puppet
14. top
15. kite
16. bubbles
17. crayons/markers
18. paint
19. paintbrush
20. puzzle
21. pail
22. shovel
23. pull toy
24. wagon
25. toy animal: dog/cat/bird/fish; farm animals

Category 2: Twenty-Five First Food Words—Activity

Objective: To help your child identify twenty-five food words

Method (e.g., the word *cookie*):

1. Present a cookie to your child.
2. Say, "cookie," "cookie."
3. Reinforce: say, "cookie."
4. Demonstrate: eat, break, feed, chew, say "cookie" while taking one out of the box.
5. Repetition: say, "cookie"; continue to demonstrate.

Steps toward understanding.

Directions: Show your child how to

1. Point to the cookie.
2. Take the cookie.
3. Give the cookie.
4. Feed the cookie to the doll.
5. Sign or say cookie.

After your child has achieved mastery you will tell your child:

1. Point to the cookie.
2. Take the cookie.
3. Give the cookie.
4. Feed the cookie to the doll.
5. Sign or say cookie.

After achieving mastery you will ask your child:

1. "What is this?" He will sign or say, "cookie."
2. Show a picture of a girl eating a cookie and ask, "What is the girl eating?"
3. Go to a bakery: point to the cookies in the display. Buy a cookie. Eat the cookie.
4. Bake cookies.

Continue this format for the remaining twenty-four food words.

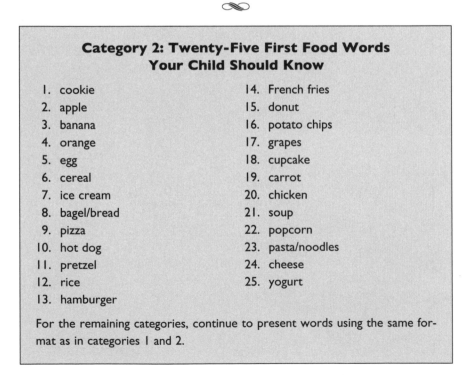

Category 2: Twenty-Five First Food Words
Your Child Should Know

1. cookie	14.	French fries
2. apple	15.	donut
3. banana	16.	potato chips
4. orange	17.	grapes
5. egg	18.	cupcake
6. cereal	19.	carrot
7. ice cream	20.	chicken
8. bagel/bread	21.	soup
9. pizza	22.	popcorn
10. hot dog	23.	pasta/noodles
11. pretzel	24.	cheese
12. rice	25.	yogurt
13. hamburger		

For the remaining categories, continue to present words using the same format as in categories 1 and 2.

Category 3: Ten First Drink Words Your Child Should Know

1. water
2. juice
3. milk
4. tea (hot/iced)
5. chocolate milk
6. hot chocolate
7. soda
8. punch
9. milkshake
10. smoothie

Category 4: Thirty First Community Worker Words Your Child Should Know

1. policeman/woman, police officer
2. fireman/woman, firefighter
3. mailman/woman, letter carrier
4. sanitation worker
5. doctor
6. nurse
7. gardener
8. teacher
9. dentist
10. barber/hairstylist
11. crossing guard
12. baker
13. butcher
14. florist
15. grocer
16. park worker
17. librarian
18. security guard
19. pilot
20. bus driver
21. train engineer
22. taxi driver
23. waiter/waitress
24. pharmacist
25. chef
26. farmer
27. lifeguard
28. gas station worker
29. president
30. clergy leader

Category 5: Thirty First Transportation Words Your Child Should Know

1. car		16. racing car
2. bus		17. sailboat
3. train		18. taxi
4. truck		19. moving truck
5. bicycle/tricycle		20. van
6. motorcycle		21. camper
7. plane		22. tractor
8. helicopter		23. golf cart
9. rocket ship		24. ice cream truck
10. boat		25. tow truck
11. canoe		26. fire truck
12. rowboat		27. police car
13. ship		28. school bus
14. tugboat		29. wagon
15. kayak		30. carriage

Category 6: Thirty-Five First Location/Place Words Your Child Should Know

1. house
2. apartment building
3. office building
4. police station
5. fire station
6. supermarket
7. fruit and vegetable store
8. pizza store
9. toy store
10. flower shop
11. butcher
12. bakery
13. drugstore/pharmacy
14. candy store
15. library
16. museum
17. circus
18. theater
19. park
20. zoo
21. beach
22. pet store
23. gas station
24. school
25. shoe store
26. farm
27. barn
28. stable
29. garden
30. house of worship
31. living room
32. kitchen
33. bathroom
34. bedroom
35. bank

Category 7: Thirty First Body Part
Words Your Child Should Know

1. head
2. hair
3. eyebrows
4. eyelashes
5. eyes
6. nose
7. chin
8. mouth/tongue
9. lips
10. teeth
11. neck
12. shoulders
13. arm
14. elbow
15. wrist
16. hand
17. finger/thumb
18. fingernail
19. chest
20. stomach/belly
21. waist
22. hips
23. legs
24. knees
25. ankle
26. foot/heel
27. toes
28. toenails
29. ears
30. face/cheeks

Category 8: Fifty First Clothing Words
Your Child Should Know

1. undershirt	26. scarf
2. underpants	27. gloves
3. socks	28. mittens
4. diaper/pull-up	29. sneakers
5. tights	30. boots
6. blouse	31. dress shoes
7. skirt	32. slippers
8. dress	33. water shoes
9. pants	34. sun hat
10. shirt	35. baseball cap
11. sweater	36. belt
12. jacket/coat	37. poncho
13. T-shirt	38. costume
14. shorts	39. jeans
15. raincoat	40. sandals
16. snowsuit	41. zipper
17. hat	42. button
18. hood	43. lace
19. sweatshirt	44. Velcro
20. sweatpants	45. hook
21. bathing suit	46. tie
22. pajamas	47. knot
23. bathrobe	48. snap
24. earmuffs	49. shoelace
25. vest	50. buckle

Category 9: Twenty-Five First Sports Words Your Child Should Know

1. basketball
2. baseball
3. football
4. soccer
5. tennis
6. swimming
7. jogging/running
8. bicycle riding/biking
9. horseback riding
10. climbing
11. table tennis/ping pong
12. yoga
13. karate
14. skiing
15. snowboarding
16. ice skating
17. rollerblading/roller skating
18. sailing
19. rowing
20. fishing
21. hockey
22. gymnastics
23. volleyball
24. golf
25. bowling

Category 10: Twenty-Five First Color and Shape Words Your Child Should Know

1. red	14. triangle
2. blue	15. rectangle
3. yellow	16. cone
4. orange	17. star
5. green	18. diamond
6. pink	19. oval
7. purple	20. cube
8. brown	21. heart
9. white	22. pyramid
10. black	23. sphere/ball/globe
11. gray	24. crescent/moon
12. circle	25. rainbow
13. square	

Category 11: Twenty First Weather and Season Words Your Child Should Know

1. sunny/sun	11. hurricane
2. cloudy/cloud	12. fog
3. windy	13. lightning
4. hot	14. thunder
5. cold	15. snowflake
6. cool	16. raindrop
7. warm	17. fall: leaves/colors/trees/fall off
8. rain/raining	18. winter: branches/empty
9. snow/snowing	19. spring: new leaves/growing/buds
10. blizzard	20. summer: leaves/flowers

Category 12: Fifty First Time
Words Your Child Should Know

1. morning	26. birthday
2. afternoon	27. year/month
3. night	28. season
4. breakfast time	29. summer
5. lunchtime	30. fall
6. dinnertime	31. winter
7. snack time	32. spring
8. daytime	33. July 4th/President's Day
9. now	34. Thanksgiving Day
10. later	35. Chanukah
11. soon	36. Christmas
12. next	37. Easter
13. today	38. Passover
14. tomorrow	39. January
15. yesterday	40. February
16. Sunday	41. March
17. Monday	42. April
18. Tuesday	43. May
19. Wednesday	44. June
20. Thursday	45. July
21. Friday	46. August
22. Saturday	47. September
23. week	48. October
24. weekend	49. November
25. time out	50. December

Category 13: Fifty First Action Words Your Child Should Know

1. eating
2. drinking
3. walking
4. running
5. hopping
6. cooking
7. pouring
8. coloring
9. writing
10. dancing
11. singing
12. washing
13. building
14. working
15. mixing
16. painting
17. throwing
18. catching
19. cutting
20. pasting
21. sleeping/playing
22. falling
23. playing
24. sitting
25. blowing
26. pulling
27. pushing
28. planting
29. digging
30. reading
31. hiding
32. sewing
33. carrying
34. laughing
35. crying
36. kicking
37. picking
38. sweeping
39. raking
40. shoveling
41. hiding
42. watching/looking
43. taking
44. giving
45. sharing
46. fixing
47. crawling
48. swimming
49. rolling
50. climbing

Category 14: Twenty-Five First Preposition Words Your Child Should Know

1. in
2. out
3. on
4. off
5. top
6. bottom
7. over
8. under
9. near
10. far
11. across
12. before
13. after
14. first
15. next
16. last
17. next to
18. behind
19. in front
20. between
21. middle
22. around
23. up
24. down
25. by

Category 15: Forty First Descriptive
Words Your Child Should Know

1. red		21. hot
2. blue		22. cold
3. green		23. crunchy
4. yellow		24. wet
5. pink		25. dry
6. brown		26. yummy
7. purple		27. near
8. black		28. far
9. white		29. empty
10. orange		30. full
11. big		31. good
12. small		32. bad
13. long		33. light
14. short		34. dark
15. thick		35. old
16. thin		36. new
17. round		37. dirty
18. square		38. clean
19. soft		39. heavy
20. hard		40. light

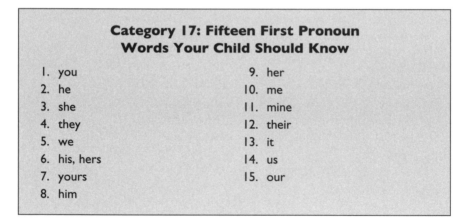

Category 16: Fifteen First Family Words Your Child Should Know

1. mommy
2. daddy
3. sister
4. brother
5. baby
6. grandma
7. grandpa
8. aunt
9. uncle
10. friend
11. neighbor
12. family
13. boy
14. girl
15. cousin

Category 17: Fifteen First Pronoun Words Your Child Should Know

1. you
2. he
3. she
4. they
5. we
6. his, hers
7. yours
8. him
9. her
10. me
11. mine
12. their
13. it
14. us
15. our

Category 18: Thirty First Fruit and Vegetable Words Your Child Should Know

1. apple
2. banana
3. orange
4. cherry/cherries
5. grapes
6. watermelon
7. melon
8. pineapple
9. tomato
10. cucumber
11. potato
12. lettuce
13. carrots
14. green beans
15. celery
16. spinach
17. beets
18. onions
19. broccoli
20. cabbage
21. peach
22. plum
23. kiwi
24. strawberry
25. blueberry
26. peppers: green, red, yellow, orange
27. radish
28. cauliflower
29. pumpkin
30. zucchini

Category 19: Forty-Five First Animal Words Your Child Should Know

1. elephant
2. zebra
3. monkey
4. kangaroo
5. lion
6. tiger
7. bear
8. polar bear
9. snake
10. giraffe
11. hippopotamus/hippo
12. whale
13. lizard
14. alligator
15. camel
16. seal
17. fish
18. dolphin
19. whale
20. crab
21. shark
22. octopus
23. turtle
24. lobster
25. clam
26. dog
27. cat
28. bird
29. fish
30. gerbil
31. hamster
32. bunny rabbit
33. lizard
34. hermit crab
35. pigeon
36. squirrel
37. deer
38. beaver
39. raccoon
40. skunk
41. owl
42. fox
43. wolf
44. chipmunk
45. frog

Category 20: Twenty-Five First Farm and Country Words Your Child Should Know

1. farm	14. barn
2. country	15. stable
3. farmer	16. pail
4. cow	17. tractor
5. milk	18. grass
6. chicken	19. pond/lake
7. eggs	20. plant
8. pig	21. seeds
9. horse	22. shovel
10. goat	23. dig
11. sheep	24. rabbit
12. hay	25. duck
13. corn	

Category 21: Twenty City Words Your Child Should Know

1. traffic light	11. newspaper stand
2. green light	12. street lights
3. red light	13. bench
4. walk go	14. mailbox
5. don't walk/stop	15. curb
6. sidewalk	16. corner
7. gutter/street	17. office building
8. fire hydrant	18. bus stop
9. sewer	19. train station
10. garbage can	20. park

Category 22: Fifteen First Entertainment Words Your Child Should Know

1. TV/television
2. games
3. cartoons
4. movies
5. computer
6. amusement park
7. roller coaster
8. merry-go-round
9. water park
10. water slide
11. Hershey Park
12. Sesame Place
13. Disney World/Land
14. rides
15. CD player/iPod

Category 23: Twenty First School Words Your Child Should Know

1. teacher
2. classroom
3. school
4. school bus
5. desk/table
6. chair
7. scissors
8. notebook
9. crayon(s)
10. pencil(s)
11. book bag
12. lunch bag
13. glue stick
14. pencil case
15. tape
16. marker(s)
17. paint
18. paintbrush
19. paper
20. play dough

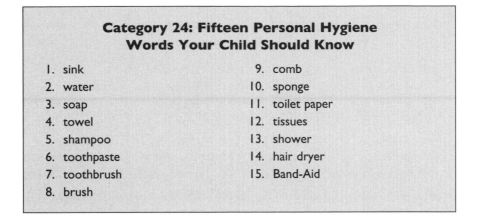

Category 24: Fifteen Personal Hygiene Words Your Child Should Know

1. sink
2. water
3. soap
4. towel
5. shampoo
6. toothpaste
7. toothbrush
8. brush
9. comb
10. sponge
11. toilet paper
12. tissues
13. shower
14. hair dryer
15. Band-Aid

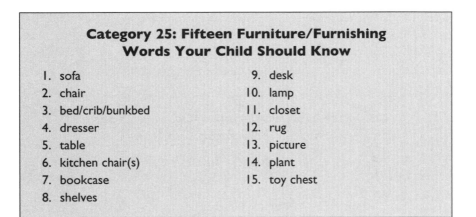

Category 25: Fifteen Furniture/Furnishing Words Your Child Should Know

1. sofa
2. chair
3. bed/crib/bunkbed
4. dresser
5. table
6. kitchen chair(s)
7. bookcase
8. shelves
9. desk
10. lamp
11. closet
12. rug
13. picture
14. plant
15. toy chest

Category 26: Twenty-Five Popular Children's Characters Your Child Should Know

1. Barbie
2. Sponge Bob
3. Bert
4. Ernie
5. Elmo
6. Big Bird
7. Cookie Monster
8. Dora
9. Diego
10. Boots
11. Woody
12. Buzz Lightyear
13. Mickey Mouse
14. Minnie Mouse
15. Donald Duck
16. Bugs Bunny
17. Cinderella
18. Belle
19. Snow White
20. Ariel/Little Mermaid
21. Jasmine
22. Thomas the Tank Engine
23. James the Red Engine
24. McQueen
25. Hello Kitty

Category 27: Twenty-Five Kitchen/Serving Words Your Child Should Know

1. fork
2. knife
3. spoon
4. plate
5. napkin
6. cereal/soup bowl
7. placemat
8. glass
9. cup
10. bottle
11. sip cup
12. straw
13. pot(s)/pan(s)
14. refrigerator
15. stove
16. oven
17. microwave
18. toaster
19. dishwasher
20. blender
21. counter
22. drawer
23. can opener
24. oven mitt/potholder
25. ice maker/ice tray

In this chapter, I have provided you with more than seven hundred words that children should know. This is not to overwhelm you but rather to inspire you to see the potential your child hopefully has.

ACTIVITY WORKSHEET
FOR SINGLE WORD
DEVELOPMENT

You now have twenty-seven categories representing over seven hundred single words. Use the following worksheet to create a vocabulary book for your child. This is very important and I strongly urge you to follow through. I create books for the children I work with, and they are very effective. Copy the worksheet and keep the pages in a binder. Find a picture for each new word your child learns and paste it on a page. Write the word on the bottom of the picture. Now your child can see the written word, associate the word with the picture, expand her knowledge about the word, and hopefully say the word. Your child will then be ready to answer questions about the word to develop comprehension. Review the book every day from the beginning if necessary. Make the book accessible to your child. Encourage your child to look at the book on her own. It will be quite rewarding to see your child in her personal space looking at the pictures, turning the pages, and saying the words. Remember, building her vocabulary will be the way to give her world meaning. It is essential.

Worksheet

Word Category: Date:

Single Word:

[paste a picture of target word or action]

Write the word under the picture.

Say the word.

Demonstrate or give examples.

Step #1: Say the word; demonstrate the word.

    Reinforce: Point to the picture, object, action, place.

    Expand the experience.

    Repetition: Repeat word.

    Demonstrate word:

    Associate word with picture, object, action, place.

    Generalize: Show the word in different contexts.

    Pretend play: Give the word more meaning.

    Carry over: Go to another location where you can learn about the word.

    Present many auditory and visual experiences to expand the idea.

    Help your child understand the concept.

Step #2: Questions: Ask questions about the word.

Answering questions appropriately demonstrates comprehension.

Sample Worksheet

Word Category: Action Word

Single Word: Drinking

[Paste a picture of the action "drinking." Consider a photograph of you or your child drinking.]

*Parent says: "What is the boy/girl doing?"

Parent rapidly answers: "Drinking."

Parent says: "What is the boy/girl doing?"

Parent rapidly answers: "Drinking."

** Parent, ask your child: "Jack, what is the boy doing?"

Wait for your child's response.

Reward any attempt at response and say, "Yes, drinking!"

Go back to **

If no response, go back to * and continue.

Use as many repetitions as necessary.

Reinforce: Stay with this action word.

Demonstrate: Have your child drink while you say, "Drinking."

Act out: You drink, saying, "What is mommy doing?" "Drinking."

Associate with the picture: "What is he/she doing?" "Drinking."

Generalize: family/friends, "What are they doing?" "Drinking."

Pretend play: use dolls/toy figures/toy cups.

Say, "What is the doll doing?" "Drinking."

Carry over: Go to a coffee shop, point out other people drinking and ask,

"What are they doing?" "Drinking."

"What is he/she doing?" "Drinking."

This format will work for the more than seven hundred words I have presented. Just adjust the questions to correspond to the context of the word.

PART THREE SUMMARY

For typically developing children, speech and language onset are automatic functions. Young children experiment with different sounds. Toward their first birthday, they zone in on the sounds of their mother tongue and begin to associate the sounds that form words. Words take on meaning, and by the age of two, children are on their way to expressing ideas and understanding what they hear. By the age of five, children's grammatical development resembles an adult's. Children talk about different ideas and interests than adults do, but subject-verb-object organization, use of plurality, tense, and other grammatical rules reach mastery. As has been the emphasis of this book, not all children develop oral language. Some children, due to hearing impairment or other developmental or neurological challenges, learn to communicate nonverbally using signs. It is important to keep in mind that Signed American English replicates the same grammatical rules as oral language. The typically developing child will learn the signing system, as well as the child who learns oral language. Our challenge is when children are not developing or using speech and language within the expected window of opportunity, or when this delay or desire to communicate interferes with social language development and interpersonal connections. In the latter situation, the employment of a different approach is required, and according to the current literature, the earlier intervention is received, the more successful the result. You the parent are now empowered to intervene. You the parent now have a strategy to activate your child's innate process of communication, which for reasons that we do not fully understand is not emerging spontaneously. You will need to both encourage and stimulate your child's willingness and desire to communicate, while at the same time help your child discover language. Helping him integrate words and actions with meaning requires a strategy that follows the experiences of typical language planning. Now you have a fund of categories and words, representing a core concept of ideas, to facilitate your child's understanding about the world, and a way to prompt interpersonal connections. Your goal is to bring meaning to your child's confusing world.

Part Four

VERBATIM SAMPLES OF SPECTRUM LANGUAGE DISORDERS

INTRODUCTION

So far I've talked about typical and disordered speech and language development, the dynamics of social communication, how to set up a language enriched home environment, how to stimulate meaningful play, and the types of toys that naturally encourage such play. I have also provided you with a collection of single words that are important for children to know, and explained how two-word combinations are formed. Now it's important for you to become familiar with the way children with language delay or at risk for ASD talk and answer questions. In order to do that, you need to have samples of what delayed children actually say. Over the course of my career, I have collected samples of verbatim transcripts that illustrate the way language delayed children talk. Why are verbatim transcripts important? In the next chapter you will learn why.

30

WHY ARE VERBATIM TRANSCRIPTS IMPORTANT?

One way of taking the mystery out of how verbal children on the spectrum communicate is by looking at real examples of what children actually say. If you learn to understand how your child thinks, you will be better able to anticipate her answers. This will help you construct your conversation and questions in a way that will promote her ability to respond in meaningful ways. Through experience you will learn what words to use and whether your message is too complex for her to process. You will learn to simplify your ideas and use pictures or visual prompts to help her gain understanding. Sometimes a visual example will make all the difference in your child's ability to sort out the confusion she is experiencing. In addition, you will realize the importance of having your child's attention in order to maximize learning and memory. You will find that many children at risk for ASD share similar deficits in communication processing.

They

- do not understand what they hear;
- answer questions by repeating words they hear last;
- repeat whole ideas they hear, which is known as echolalia;
- repeat words or ideas many times in a row, even ideas from the past, which is known as perseveration;
- are very concrete thinkers;
- do not understand *wh* concepts: who, when, where, why; and

- do not understand children's stories. Keep in mind that even though storybooks are written for young children, the dialogue between the characters, vocabulary, and level of abstraction is often far too complex for the child at risk to comprehend.

Higher functioning children who attend mainstream inclusion programs often have significant difficulty with

- understanding social conversation between children;
- getting jokes, riddles, abstract ideas;
- understanding the feelings of others;
- realizing the consequences of their behavior;
- comprehending what they read, since they may not adequately understand the characters and plot line; and
- understanding homonyms, words that sound the same but have different meanings.

High functioning children are also concrete thinkers and find it difficult if not impossible to read between the lines. They see the world through their own point of view and have little if any common sense.

Example: Once, I was working with a high functioning, mainstream eight-year-old diagnosed with ASD. We were going to work on an expressive writing assignment. I handed her a piece of paper and told her we were going to write a letter. Within a moment she handed the paper back to me. "Here," she said. She wrote a letter of the alphabet.

The following chapters offer verbatim samples, giving you a valuable opportunity to see how children at risk think and communicate in real time. Once you understand the core language deficits of ASD you will be able to communicate and help your child more effectively. This will give you greater confidence and opportunity to help your child break through the language barrier. Now I will introduce you to a child I worked with and how he *actually* processed language.

CASE HISTORY

Justin, Two Years, Three Months Old

History: At 2 years, 3 months of age, Justin was diagnosed with pervasive developmental delay (PDD), at risk for ASD.

At the time of the early intervention evaluation, the speech therapist reported the following about Justin:

- Does not use words, sounds, or gestures to indicate wants.
- He tries to get by, by himself.
- Responds to "give me" and "clean up," but no other directions.
- Does not understand what he does not see.
- Knows animal sounds and will make them if you ask.
- Plays a "where are you" game and will run away to be found.
- Is very active.
- Is beginning to make motions to familiar songs.
- Has about twenty-five words.
- Can identify some common objects from pictures.
- Does not understand colors nor match colors or objects.
- Has a short attention span, strong willed.
- Behavior is erratic.

Early intervention recommendations:

- Center-based services five days a week.
- Occupational therapy three times a week.
- Special instruction five times a week, center based.
- Special instruction ten hours a week at home.
- Speech therapy five times a week in school additional therapy outside of school.

In the next chapter you will find a summary of ten therapy sessions with Justin, that span from 4 years, 3 months to 4 years, 10 months of age. Each session will be followed by an explanation of his responses, to give you more insight.

32

TRANSCRIPTS FOR JUSTIN

The following series of language samples is being presented with the intention of having you experience the way Justin, a child at risk for ASD, thinks and processes conversation in a variety of contexts. These samples are not to be construed as the way all children at risk for ASD think, but rather they will give you a feel for how a child at risk may think, and in particular how Justin does think. Justin's replies are *actual verbatim transcripts and not made-up instances*. Pretend you are the paratherapist. As you read the transcripts try to identify which responses are echolalic and perseverative, which are irrelevant to the topic, and which are meaningful. These samples will illustrate the language challenges, and barriers, Justin experiences. In addition, this section will provide you with a language sample format. You will be able to use the same format in order to record samples of your own child's responses, allowing you to analyze and evaluate her ideas, just as you will for Justin.

You will now review ten verbatim transcripts, recorded during therapy with Justin over a seven-month period of time.

#1: Justin: 4 years, 3 months: The Birthday Cake

Words: birthday, party, cake, candles, balloons, bakery, baker
Activity: Listening to a story about Bill's birthday
Talk about/retell the story
Pretend party with party goods
Therapist reads a short story with illustration:

Therapist reads: "This is a boy named Bill, and his mother.
It's Bill's birthday.
They are going to buy a birthday cake."
[Bill and his mother]

THERAPIST	CHILD
1. "What is the boy's name?" → [the story is reread]	"birthday"
2. "What is the boy's name?" →	"boy"
3. "What is the boy's name?" → [more discussion about the story]	"mother"
4. "What is the boy's name?" →	"boy"
5. "What are they going to buy?" →	"food"
6. "Who is in the story?" →	"buy, birthday cake"

Justin could not identify Bill's name or mother when asked questions about them. Justin was having significant difficulty paying attention to the story. He did not listen and focus on the task in order to keep the information active in his mind. It appears that he did process that they were going to buy a birthday cake. The word *buy* was associated with food, and then correctly associated with birthday cake. This is a good example of how attention interferes with language processing. Justin's selective recall caused him to fail to identify names. The same was not true about the cake. Putting the story into picture format will help improve his selective recall.

∞

#2: Justin: 4 years, 3 months: The Cook

Words: cook, soup, pot, spoon, stove, cooking, mixing
Activity: Pretend cooking in the kitchen, toy vegetables, toy pots and pans
Listening to a short story/answer questions

Story: "This is the cook
He is making/cooking soup.
He needs a pot."

THERAPIST	CHILD
1. "Who is he?" [pointing to the cook] →	"bakery"
2. "What is he doing?" →	"making cookie and cakes"
3. "Where are the cookies and the cake?" →	"in the pot"
4. "Are we making cookies and cake in the pot?" →	"yeah"
5. "Look at the picture, what is he holding? →	"a pot"
6. "What is he making in the pot?" →	"soup"
7. "Right, there are no cookies in the pot, what is he making?" →	"he's gonna make a pot, it's going to be very hot"

Justin is still thinking about Bill and the birthday cake, from the other day. He is associating cooking with baking cookies and cakes. Yet with pictures and pretend play Justin is able to redirect. In line 5 he identifies that the cook is holding the pot, and that he is making soup. The message in line 7 becomes a little too complex for him to process. He confuses the words: he's gonna make a pot, instead of make soup; however, he knows that the soup will be very hot. This is a good example of how children at risk for ASD perseverate on what they selectively remember from the past. With visual and hands-on experiences, as well as being more focused, Justin was able to be redirected.

∞

#3: Justin: 4 years, 3 months: The Alligator

Justin was interested in the toy alligator.
Goal: To talk about the alligator.
Look at an alligator picture book.
Color in the alligator coloring book.
Words: alligator, green, land, water, swim, walk, eat
Activity: Justin plays with the alligator, looks at an alligator book and alligator coloring book.

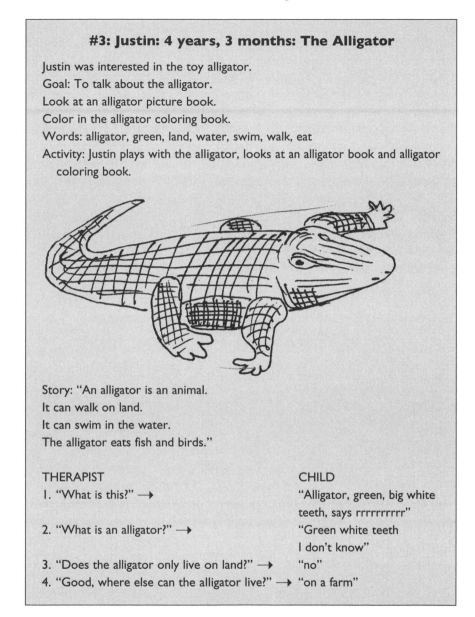

Story: "An alligator is an animal.
It can walk on land.
It can swim in the water.
The alligator eats fish and birds."

THERAPIST	CHILD
1. "What is this?" →	"Alligator, green, big white teeth, says rrrrrrrrrr"
2. "What is an alligator?" →	"Green white teeth I don't know"
3. "Does the alligator only live on land?" →	"no"
4. "Good, where else can the alligator live?" →	"on a farm"

Justin enjoyed playing with the alligator. His answers are more relevant and descriptive compared to other samples. For question 1 he correctly answers that the animal is an alligator and that it is green. Although his grammatical development is delayed with errors in word order, he is willing to give more details. He uses two descriptive words to describe the alligator's teeth, and added that it roars. He is more engaged and conversational. His attention is better and he is socially involved. For question 2 Justin begins to perseverate about the green white teeth, but then refocuses. He does not know that an alligator is an animal. He remembers that the alligator can live in the water and on the land, but for question 4 he answers that it also lives on a farm. His response is important for two reasons: (1) He answered the where question correctly. A farm is a place. (2) Although irrelevant, we talked about the farm in the past. He remembers being asked, where does the [cow, etc.] live, and overgeneralizes the question. He remembers an experience about where animals live, and selectively chooses farm. This dialogue is a good example of (1) how a motivating subject, with fun toys, pictures, and activities increases attention, focus, socialization, and understanding, and (2) how Justin is having difficulty organizing past words and experiences in his memory for later recall, and (3) how Justin knows the word *alligator*, but does not understand the category word *animal*.

∞

#4: Justin 4 years, 3 months: Alligator Eggs

Goal: To continue talking about the alligator.

Words: alligator, eggs, baby

Activity: Since Justin was interested in the alligator we will continue to play and talk about baby alligators. The original story about the alligator is re-read. We talk about the story to help with recall.

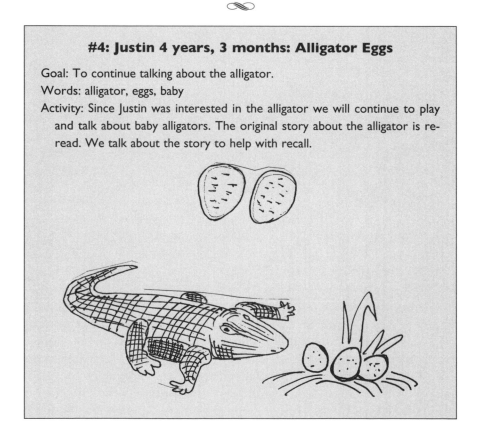

New story: "The mommy alligator lays eggs.
She will have baby alligators."

THERAPIST	CHILD
1. "What is in the eggs?" →	"chicks"
2. "Can an alligator swim?" →	"no"
3. "What does he do on land?" →	"in the water"

I did not expect Justin to answer that chicks were in the eggs. Concerned that he was still selecting ideas from his farm experience, the questions were redirected to talk about the grown alligator from the previous therapy session. For question 2 he answers no, about the alligator being able to swim. He does not attend to question 3, remains selectively focused on the word *swim*, and answers "in the water." This is a good example of how ASD impacts on memory, auditory processing, and organization of ideas. It also shows the importance of repetition, since it takes many experiences for words and ideas to be understood and recalled. Ongoing relearning is an important goal for Justin.

#5: Justin 4 years, 4 months: The Rainy Day

Goal: Conversation about a rainy day.

Analyzing a rainy day picture.

Words: rain, raining, clouds, sky, umbrella, boots, raincoat, rain hat, duck, puddle

Activity: Let's look at the picture. We can talk about what we see. Use figures of people to pretend they are outside in the rain. Make paper boots, raincoat, rain hat, umbrella.

THERAPIST	CHILD
1. "Is this a sunny day or a rainy day?" →	"rainy"
2. "How do you know? →	"because he's holding umbrella and has a hat"
3 "Tell me more." →	"because she has a raincoat"
4. "Why does she need a raincoat?" →	"for rain, swimming"
5. "Where does the rain come from?" →	"from the duck"
6. "Where does the rain come from?" →	"the picture, from a boots, down there"

Justin was able to attend, process, and stay on topic for the first three questions of the conversation. He has confusion with who is wearing the rain hat, and he/she pronoun identification. By question 4 he starts making word associations off-topic. By question 5 his ability to answer the question in a meaningful way declines. When question 5 is repeated his answers become very concrete. Looking at the picture of the rainy scene, he concludes that the rain comes from the picture, then the boots, then down there. Justin shows that he is trying to identify a place where the rain comes from. This is a good example of language processing confusion for both understanding the question, and recalling a meaningful answer. Each idea needs to be presented separately with pictures and visual aids. Here are some examples to be worked on: clouds are in the sky and rain comes/falls from the clouds; we hold an umbrella when it rains to keep dry; we wear a raincoat, rain hat, boots in the rain to stay dry; the duck is swimming in the puddle; ducks like water.

∽

#6: At 4 years, 5 months: Going Shopping

Goal: To talk about the day Danny went shopping
Words: store, food, grocery, supermarket, shopping cart
Activity: Pretend to be shopping, with shopping cart, toy food, pretend money.

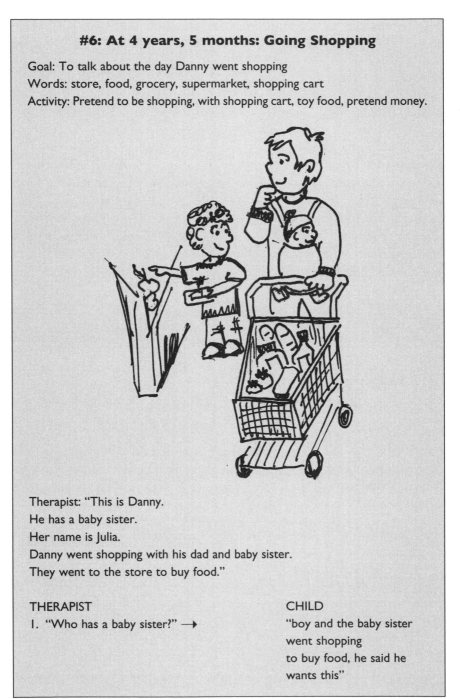

Therapist: "This is Danny.
He has a baby sister.
Her name is Julia.
Danny went shopping with his dad and baby sister.
They went to the store to buy food."

THERAPIST	CHILD
1. "Who has a baby sister?" →	"boy and the baby sister went shopping to buy food, he said he wants this"

2. "What is his sister's name?" →	"he's gonna buy banana I like banana with soup and cheese"
3. "Where did Danny go?" →	"he went to buy banana, I like banana banana with soup and cheese"
4. "Who took Danny and Julia shopping?" →	"to buy banana and eat it with soup and cheese, it's snowing outside"

From the pretend play experience and listening to the story, Justin was able to recall the main idea, about shopping for food. He was unable to answer the questions because he was self-absorbed, talking about the banana, soup, and cheese. He was not focusing on the questions, nor processing the words. He could not be redirected in order to stop his perseverative conversation. This is a good example of how a child at risk for ASD perseverates on an idea. This experience is not productive.

#7: At 4 years, 5 months: The Dishwasher

Goal: Using a word and concept meaningfully
Talking about the kitchen
Word: dishwasher
Concept: washes dishes, makes dishes clean, soap, water
Activity: pretend play, washing dirty dishes
Short story with two facts

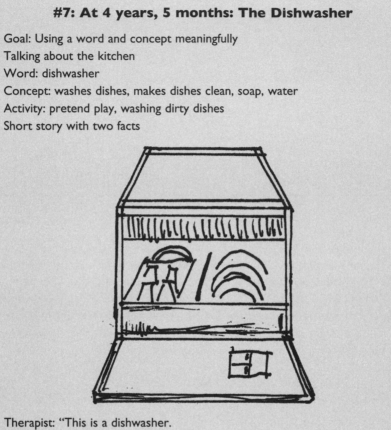

Therapist: "This is a dishwasher.
This machine washes dirty dishes."

THERAPIST	CHILD
1. "What is this?" →	"It's called January, February, March, December"
2. "What does the dishwasher do?" →	"for make food, for making a night to make it hot"
3. "What do you put inside the dishwasher?" →	"to make it hot"

The response to question 1 is irrelevant, and is attributed to the child's lack of attention at the beginning of the session.

The responses to questions 2 and 3 appear irrelevant until the clarification by the mother. The door of the oven and the door of the dishwasher open the same way. The child associates the dishwasher with the oven. The mother explained that she cooks at night, and says "the oven is hot."

As a result, from the child's experiences he has seen his mother make food, at night, in the hot oven.

It is common for children at risk for ASD to formulate overgeneralized concrete concepts. Since the dishwasher and oven open the same way, until further learning takes place, the dishwasher may be confused as the oven.

Goals would be for the child to

- understand different uses and functions of machines and appliances,
- improve grammatical form, and
- improve vocabulary.

#8: At 4 years, 10 months: The Dishwasher—
Follow-up therapy session

Five months later
Goal: Using a word and concept meaningfully
Concept: washes dishes
Activity: pretend play, washing dirty dishes

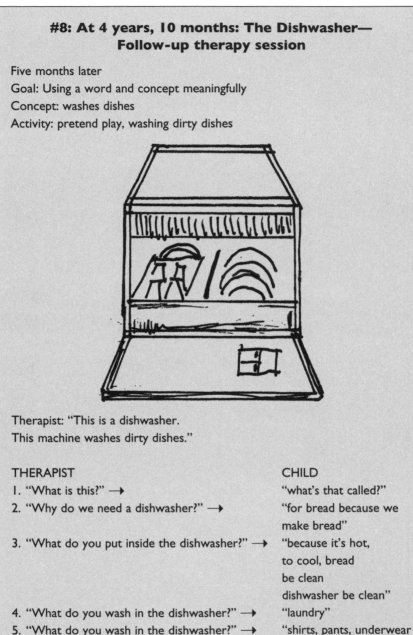

Therapist: "This is a dishwasher.
This machine washes dirty dishes."

THERAPIST	CHILD
1. "What is this?" →	"what's that called?"
2. "Why do we need a dishwasher?" →	"for bread because we make bread"
3. "What do you put inside the dishwasher?" →	"because it's hot, to cool, bread be clean dishwasher be clean"
4. "What do you wash in the dishwasher?" →	"laundry"
5. "What do you wash in the dishwasher?" →	"shirts, pants, underwear "dishwasher, bread"

This follow-up lesson has shown little progress due to considerable auditory processing confusion. The word, concept, and function for dishwasher are too complex, causing significant misunderstanding. Focus is being placed on the word *wash*. Now wash is being associated with laundry, and responses are out of context.

Continue to learn the name, use, and function of various machines and appliances.

Minimize confusion between dishwasher and dishes, from washing machine and clothes.

∞

#9: At 4 years 5 months: The Refrigerator

Goal: using a word and concept meaningfully
Words: refrigerator, kitchen, food
Concept: cold, kitchen, foods found in the refrigerator
Activity: pretend play with toy refrigerator/kitchen, toy foods, pictures
Short story with three facts

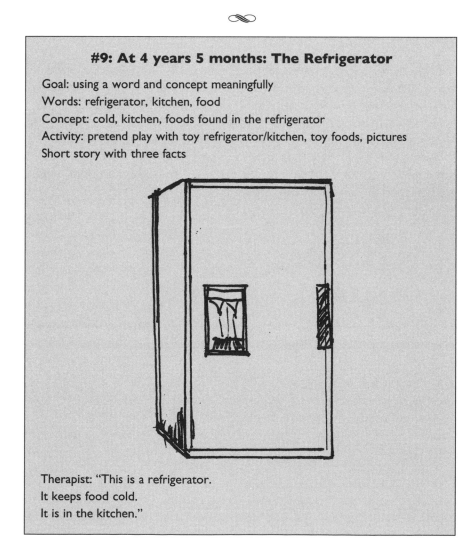

Therapist: "This is a refrigerator.
It keeps food cold.
It is in the kitchen."

THERAPIST	CHILD
1. "What is this?" →	"milk, cups, choco"
	[pointing to refrigerator]
2. "Why do we need a refrigerator?" →	"food and the cups"
3. "Why do we keep food in the	
refrigerator?" →	"in the bathtub"
4. "How does the refrigerator feel inside?" →	"cups and pita bread"
5. "Why do we keep food in the	
refrigerator? →	"to fall asleep
	It's time to call 911, and . . ."

From the dialogue you can see that Justin is having significant difficulty processing the questions, especially questions 3 and 5. The questions may have become too complex, causing a breakdown in understanding.

However, in response to questions 1, 2, and 4 he apparently zoned in on the word *refrigerator* and responded with drink words: milk, choco [for chocolate milk], and cup. He also responded with "food" and "pita bread." Although his answers are not meaningful, he is making associations, which is a good and positive step.

Suggested goals: to learn

1. name for refrigerator
2. we keep food inside
3. it is cold
4. drinks and words for some refrigerator foods
5. where the refrigerator is located

To answer questions to demonstrate understanding:

1. What is this? [refrigerator]
2. What do we keep inside the refrigerator? [cold foods, drinks]
3. How does the refrigerator feel inside?
4. Where do we keep_____? [milk, juice, eggs, cheese, yogurt]
5. Why do we keep milk, juice, eggs, cheese, yogurt in the refrigerator? [to stay cold]
6. Where is the refrigerator? [in the kitchen]
7. What room is the refrigerator in? [in the kitchen]

8. Yes/No
   a. Is this a stove? [while pointing to a refrigerator]
   b. Does the refrigerator feel cold?
   c. Does the stove feel cold?
   d. Do we keep shoes in the refrigerator?
   e. Do we cook in the refrigerator?
   f. Do we keep milk in the stove?

#10: At 4 years, 10 months: The Refrigerator— Follow-up therapy session

Five months later
Goal: using a word and concept meaningfully
Concept: cold, kitchen, foods found in the refrigerator
Activity: pretend play with toy refrigerator/kitchen, toy foods, pictures

THERAPIST	CHILD
1. "What is this?" →	"refrigerator"
2. "Why do we need a refrigerator?" →	"for food, apple, tomato, apple juice, salad, cucumber"

3. "Why do we keep food in the
   refrigerator?" →   "because be food,
                                                     inside the refrigerator"

4. "Why do we keep food in the
   refrigerator?" →   "because we open and
                                                     close refrigerator,
                                                     because we buy tomato,
                                                     milk, cola, carrots,
                                                     broccoli, nothing else"

5. "Where is the refrigerator?" →   "over here"
   [in reference to the house]   [points to the picture]
6. "Where is the refrigerator?" →   "in my house"
7. "Where in your house?" →   "refrigerator"
8. "Where in your house?" →   "by the kitchen"

Five-month follow-up shows responses significantly more relevant. The child
knows the word for refrigerator when asked, "What is this?"
Right now the child has a generalized concept of the refrigerator:
a place where you keep food, and you can open and close the door.
He still lacks its function: a place that is cold, for cold foods.
Processed the *where* question: refrigerator in kitchen.
With continued repetition and experience, progress for the future is promising.

PART FOUR SUMMARY

By now you are an informed parent. You know about typical and disordered speech and language development; you know how to set up a learning space in your home and which toys to buy to create a language enriched environment; in addition you have over seven hundred important words to bring meaning into your child's very confusing world. You have acquired many facts and gained valuable knowledge.

But facts and knowledge alone are not enough. I believe that parents can only be confident when they have a sample of what a disorder *looks* like. Although there are no pictures to illustrate the characteristics of a language disorder, analyzing verbatim samples of how children choose and use words is telling. By studying real examples of what language learning disabled children actually say, you learn to understand and even anticipate how children will respond to questions and express their world. Be sure to go over the samples again and try to understand what's going wrong. Review the processing errors, and think about what could be the cause of the breakdown in communication. If your child is verbal but her responses are echolalic, or irrelevant to the topic, think about how you can promote meaning. Keep language samples of what your child talks about, and how she answers questions. Analyze the words she uses, the number of words she uses, and the appropriateness of her responses. Over time these samples will be able to help you assess progress as well as target new goals. More importantly, you will learn to understand your child much better.

Part Five

HOW TO NATURALLY ADVANCE YOUR CHILD'S COMMUNICATION DEVELOPMENT WITHOUT MISSING VALUABLE OPPORTUNITIES

INTRODUCTION

CASE HISTORY: OLD TESTAMENT, THE BOOK OF EXODUS/MOSES GOES TO SPEAK TO PHARAOH

Name: Moses
Age: 80 years old

G-d instructs Moses to go to the Pharaoh and tell him to free the Hebrew slaves from Egypt. Moses turns down the assignment, and tells G-d that he just isn't the right man for the job. Now, I could think of many reasons why Moses would feel unqualified for the post. Leading six hundred thousand people is not exactly an easy task. Maybe he felt that he didn't have the proper training, or that he didn't have a high enough rank to negotiate with a Pharaoh. What reason did Moses give to G-d?

"I am not a man of words, not since yesterday, nor since the day before yesterday, nor since You first spoke to Your servant, for I am heavy of mouth and heavy of speech." (Exodus 4:10)

Moses, because of his communication impairment, says *No* to G-d. But G-d doesn't listen. The opportunity is now, and Moses is the man. G-d isn't missing this opportunity, and he doesn't.

33

WHY IS THIS RELEVANT?

Let's rerun the script. Moses has a communication impairment that causes him to be defiant and oppositional, but G-d won't accept this behavior. A miracle could have easily solved Moses's problem, but there was no miracle. G-d wasn't giving up on Moses.

Now, let's change the cast. Your child is delayed in language development or at risk for ASD; she's defiant and oppositional. You won't accept the status quo. You decide to be proactive.

What should you do? Expose her to as many meaningful opportunities as you can to help her challenge her barriers. Don't miss the simple, valuable opportunities that wait.

What opportunities am I referring to? Everyday living activities: shopping at the supermarket, fruit and vegetable store, bakery, deli; the florist, shoe store, post office, library, clothing store, pet shop, small restaurant. At home: cooking, baking, cleaning, laundry, setting the table, clearing the table, watering plants, feeding the dog, opening the mail, putting stamps on letters, making the bed, packing an overnight bag, making lunch/packing a lunch. These are all opportunities to build language and increase knowledge. The problem as I see it is that all too often the delayed child does not participate enough. These are missed opportunities to learn.

I fully understand that behavior and transitions may at times be so disruptive that it would be next to impossible to include your child in many of these opportunities. If this is so, your first and immediate goal is to make behavior management the priority. Once you have learned effective techniques from a behavioral psychologist or ABA specialist, you will have strategies to help manage your child's conduct more productively. This will enable you to move forward, allowing you to include her in daily living experiences. She needs opportunities to naturally develop and socialize just like the typically developing child. I don't expect you to take your child everywhere you go, nor do I expect you to have her involved in everything you do. What I do want you to do is create small segments of time, in five- to ten-minute intervals, multiple times during the day, where your child can participate and be exposed to meaningful experiences. These experiences may be the key to stimulating her language, understanding, and willingness to speak. As she gains more knowledge and words you may find her functioning on a higher level than anticipated. Opportunities in life are essential. Do not allow behavior to become a harmful barrier. In the next chapter I will talk about how children miss valuable opportunities.

34

MISSED OPPORTUNITIES

Children with special needs miss opportunities all the time. I'm not talking about missing opportunities that are beyond their reach, I'm talking about opportunities they are capable of completing independently or with some supervision, opportunities where they can have a role. You have read how important experience is to learning and language development. Children with language delay or at risk for ASD need as much exposure as possible to gain knowledge about the world. Still, they don't have enough opportunity. Although it is extremely labor intensive, and at times frustrating, involving your child in everyday experiences is essential. I'm not recommending random activities but rather an organized schedule and a series of experiences each day. Using this strategy, your child has an opportunity to learn about the world via objects and events, interact with others, and have a sense of what is happening and why. You don't have to do this yourself. With an organized plan you can increase opportunities by having people you trust help.

All too often, children are placed before a screen, whether computer or television, for hours, in order to be kept busy, contained, or amused. At a family or group activity, dinner, or party, how often are special needs children included? At this point you may take exception to what I am saying, "We always take Jill with us; she's always included." Stop and think for a minute. Is she *there*, or is she *included*? In my experience special needs children are really not included. They are often not spoken to or spoken to very minimally. I have listened to grown-ups speak to special needs children; this is what they say, "good job; no, don't do that; stop that; time out; you're not going to get candy if you don't stop; don't touch; sit nicely; we're going in a minute." These are not ways to develop meaningful experiences or social skills.

Also, special needs children are almost never told where they are going or what is happening next. There isn't any "preview" of what to expect. This is especially difficult for children who have difficulty with change. Not only is life confusing and possibly scary, it's a never-ending cycle of surprises and sudden changes. Imagine playing and suddenly someone whisks you away, bundles you up, belts you into a car seat and drives away. No explanation. When you think about it, that doesn't generate secure feelings. It shouldn't be this way. Later in this section, I am going to show you how to set up a daily routine using a picture schedule. Although you are not expected to rigidly follow the same schedule every day, allowing your child to have an idea of what to expect can give her some sense of control and in turn stabilize behavior. Just by knowing the general sequence of events of a typical day may help your child make easier transitions. For example, let's pretend your child likes going to the park. From the picture schedule, she knows that it is an activity done midmorning between dressing and lunch. Knowing that after the morning routine she will get her chance to play on the swings may encourage her to be more cooperative. Knowing what is going to happen by implementing a picture schedule will help avoid the mystery of day-to-day activities.

I have just discussed the importance of giving your child opportunities to experience and learn about the world. Once the challenges of behavior are under control, your child will be better prepared to participate in everyday activities. I have shown you how children with special needs are often left out, despite the fact that they may be with you. But most concerning, children with special needs have little to no idea of what to expect during their day. In the next chapter, I am going to discuss the research of Dominic Gullo and Jeanne Gullo, referred to as "an ecological approach." You will use their philosophy as your guide to give your child daily opportunities while building language concepts and social communication.

35

GULLO AND GULLO

An Ecological Approach

I remember when I first read the article by Dominic Gullo and Jeanne Gullo in the July 1984 issue of *Language Speech and Hearing Services in Schools*. At the time, I found their research on language development important, sensible, and necessary. I incorporated their approach in therapy as well as into the curriculum of the graduate course I taught at Brooklyn College. Decades later, their research remains practical and valuable. I want to share their approach with you.

The philosophy is referred to as an *ecological* language approach. By employing natural settings, the goal is to integrate language and social development. The ecological framework consists of everyday activities and typical experiences to encourage functional communication.

In their research, the Gullos refer to the child as the "language learner." Your child is the language learner. While engaged in an everyday activity, the language learner is able to create picture images in his mind of the actions he is experiencing and the objects he is using. Actions and objects become linked to words. Words include nouns, verbs, adjectives, adverbs, and prepositions. Over time, the single word is expanded to express a thought. To broaden knowledge, words can be classified, categorized, and expressed in a sequence of ideas. While engaged in action, pragmatic skills can naturally develop. Since the activities are everyday experiences, this approach allows you to include your child in your typical routines to promote language with understanding.

The ecological approach has four key principles:

1. Language acquisition should occur in the most natural environment within a meaningful setting.
2. Language learning is a developmental process, so it is recommended to begin at the nonverbal level and advance.
3. A principal resource is the involvement of adults, and children naturally, around the language learner. This may include, but is not limited to, the teacher, child's caretaker, babysitter, or peers. This broadens your child's opportunity to interact with a greater range of people.
4. Typical language development requires active participation. Initiating or encouraging social communication, stressing words in the context of the event, and asking questions are all part of the experience.

Your goal, as the parent, is to create experiences in meaningful settings. You are going to select a vocabulary of target words that relate to the experience. While engaged in the activity you will encourage social interaction to increase your child's opportunity to be exposed to words and actions in context. In turn, this will give your child more to know about and more to talk about.

In the next chapter, I will give you a sample of an ecological language experience.

36

AN ECOLOGICAL LANGUAGE EXPERIENCE

This language experience is a great, organized way to expose your child to a natural and meaningful opportunity. Just decide to include your child in one of your daily routines. What is most worthwhile about this experience is that you are being given a recipe, or structure to follow. You can plan all the important words and directions you want to include.

Sample A: Helping with the Laundry— Understanding a Routine Experience

Who: Your child will help with the laundry.

What: Clothing, towels
Laundry basket
Detergent/soap/fabric softener
Washing machine/dryer
Clothesline/clothespins
Measuring cup

Where: Laundromat [you will need coins or a money card]
Home laundry room

Target Vocabulary:

Nouns	Verbs	Adjectives	Adverbs	Prepositions
socks	take	dirty	fast	in
underpants	put	wet	slowly	out
T-shirts	give	dry		on
pants	pour	clean		under
undershirts	open			over
towels	close			next to
washcloths	wait			on top
washing machine	fold			
soap	watch			
water	spin			
bubbles	push			
	turn			
	wash			
	tumble			

Word expansion through narration: While doing the laundry, narrate what is happening so your child will hear and see your actions in context. Make sure to use the target vocabulary words. Narrate your child's actions as well. "Jackie, you are putting the towels in." You will base the length of your narration upon your child's ability to listen and understand. Ask your child questions, and reward words or any appropriate nonverbal actions.

Narration:
"We wash clothes/laundry."
[noun + verb + noun]

"Put the laundry in the basket."
[verb + noun + preposition + noun]

Narrate what Jill is doing:
"Jill is putting the laundry in the basket."
[noun + verb + noun + preposition + noun]
"Dirty clothes!"
[adjective + plural noun]

"Put the *socks* in."
[verb + plural noun + preposition]

"Put the *shirts* in."
[verb + plural noun + preposition]

"Put the *towels* in."
[verb + plural noun + preposition]

Narrate what Jill is doing:
"Jill is putting the socks in the basket." or
"Jill is putting the shirts in the basket."
"Clothes go in the washing machine."
[noun + verb + proposition + noun]

Narrate what Jill is doing:
"Jill is putting the clothes in the washing machine." or
"Jill puts clothes in the machine."
"Put soap in."
[verb + noun + preposition]

Narrate what Jill is doing:
"Jill is putting the soap in the washing machine." or
"Jill puts soap in the machine."

Continue to narrate what you are doing.
Continue to narrate what your child is doing.
Simplify the number of words you use, based upon your child's understanding.

Following directions: Narrating directions helps with the sequence of events
    and concepts of time.
First we get the laundry.
Jill, help put the laundry in the basket.
Next let's take the laundry to the laundromat/laundry room.
Now we will make piles.
Jill, give me the towel/Jill, get the towel/Jill, put the towel here.
Jill, open the washing machine door.
Now the towels go in the washing machine. Jill, put all the towels in.
Jill, get the soap.
Let's put some soap in the cup.
Jill, hold the cup. Jill, pour the soap here.
Last, we will turn on the machine.
Continue until clothes are folded and put into drawers.

Sample B: Making Potato Latkes (potato pancakes)

Who: You and your child will make potato pancakes.

Where: Kitchen

Target Vocabulary:

Nouns	Verbs	Adjectives	Adverbs	Prepositions
potatoes	peel	hot	slowly	in
salt	cut	big	carefully	on top
flour	measure	round		
oil	mix	yummy		
pepper	blend	delicious		
baking powder	grate			
onions	smell			
eggs	taste			
bowl	pour			
fry pan	eat			
fork/spoon	serve			
potato peeler	cook/cooking			
applesauce	crack/cracking			

Word expansion through narration: While cooking potato pancakes, narrate the steps as you follow the recipe. You want your child to hear your words and see your hands in action. Make sure to use the target vocabulary words.

Narrate your child's actions as well:

"Jackie, you are mixing the potatoes," "cracking eggs, pouring oil."

You will base the length of your narration upon your child's ability to listen and understand. Ask your child questions, and reward words or any appropriate nonverbal actions.

Narration:

"Jackie, we are going to make potato pancakes."

"Put the bowl on the table/counter."

"Count the potatoes."

"Grate the potatoes."

"Grate the onions."

"Blend/mix the salt, flour, baking powder."

Make your own plan for different activities. You don't have to complete an entire task with your child. You can include her in any part you like. Remember you can apply any activity to this model. A little preplanning for target words and materials, along with some creativity, can have your child building rock gardens, planting, or setting up an aquarium. Handcrafts are also good activities for the ecological approach. Children's needlepoint, making jewelry, making potholders, stringing beads, and even creating a scrapbook are good choices. You will be able to help your child follow instructions, pay attention, improve eye contact, and follow a sequence of tasks, while you are narrating language in context.

Here is a sample form for a language experience. Follow the format, make copies, and add to your binder.

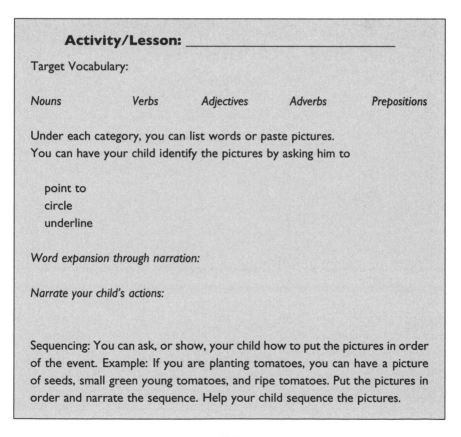

Activity/Lesson: _____

Target Vocabulary:

Nouns   *Verbs*   *Adjectives*   *Adverbs*   *Prepositions*

Under each category, you can list words or paste pictures.
You can have your child identify the pictures by asking him to

    point to
    circle
    underline

Word expansion through narration:

Narrate your child's actions:

Sequencing: You can ask, or show, your child how to put the pictures in order of the event. Example: If you are planting tomatoes, you can have a picture of seeds, small green young tomatoes, and ripe tomatoes. Put the pictures in order and narrate the sequence. Help your child sequence the pictures.

Now that you have ideas to promote language, and a way to include your child, it is time to set up a picture schedule. As I stated earlier, having a general routine with picture prompts allows your child to know what to expect during a typical day. Imagine being in a situation where you didn't know what was going to happen next. It's not a very comforting feeling. Now project this instability onto your child. A picture schedule will help to eliminate sudden changes in routine and remove surprises. Hopefully, this will make transitions easier, and behavioral outbursts less frequent. Your child may be more willing to cooperate when she knows what to expect in advance. For example, seeing the bath picture on the day's schedule may help to make the experience more positive. When children are cooperative they are more focused and productive. With this productive attitude you may be able to have your child get her towel, bring her pajamas, or choose a bath toy to play with. Without behavioral distractions there is room for learning, gaining knowledge, and understanding: the foundation of meaningful communication. In the next chapter I will give you some ideas about setting up a picture schedule.

(37)

THE PICTURE TIME SCHEDULE

Children with ASD have difficulty with change and transitions. It may be because they don't know what to expect, don't understand time, and don't have a concept of sequential events. We automatically fit our lives into the phases of a day: morning, afternoon, evening, and their relationship to breakfast, lunch, and dinner. Children with ASD don't have the same perception. They don't know, nor are they able to anticipate, what will happen; nor do they understand what will happen next. The abrupt change from one situation to the next with little to no preparation time is probably more the rule than the exception. Things just happen.

You are going to make a picture schedule. Having a picture time schedule serves two positive purposes. One, it gives your child an opportunity to learn more about her world. She will see the picture on the time schedule and associate it with the event. She will develop an understanding of what the picture defines and may begin to learn independent skills. For example, if the picture is of the park, your child may get his coat, shoes, and the ball he likes to play with. If the picture is of bath time, your child may independently go to get a towel, his pajamas, or a robe. If he doesn't initiate these actions you can ask your child to get a towel. Every time he successfully follows your directive the language process is advancing.

The second advantage is it may help with behavior. If your child has an understanding of what comes next, reaction to change and transitions may become easier. Antisocial behavior may be reduced or even eliminated. In fact, your child may begin to look forward to an activity on the schedule.

You don't have to be an artist to make the schedule; all you need is an artist's sketch pad, colored markers, photos or pictures, and a clothespin. Divide the paper into three sections from top to bottom, representing the three phases of the day. Next to the left edge of the page draw or paste pictures of the day's routines. If your child is helping with the laundry, watering plants around the house, or setting the table, have a picture to represent the activity.

In the morning, when your child wakes up, picture 1 should be of his bathroom routine. Clip a clothespin next to the picture. He needs to find the clothespin, look at the picture, and follow through on the activity. When he's finished, he needs to return to the schedule and move the clothespin to the next picture. If it's dressing, he should dress; if it's breakfast, he should eat breakfast, and so on throughout the day. Moving the clothespin will be important. At the beginning you will do this with your child, explain what you just finished and what will happen next. As time goes by, hopefully he will be able to work with the schedule more independently. Encourage him to say or repeat what he is supposed to do or where you are going. This is an important step to help your child learn about his world and understand the many events and changes that take place during a typical day.

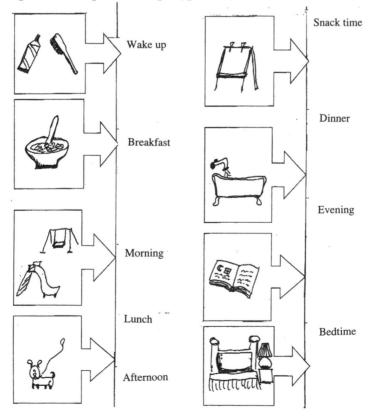

FINAL SUMMARY

At the time of this publication, the Centers for Disease Control and Prevention report that autism occurs in 1 out of 88 births, an increase from 1 out of 150 births just ten years ago. A more troubling statistic is that autism occurs in boys at a rate of 1 out of every 54 births, five times more common than among girls. To date, there is no definitive cause that answers the many questions related to this broad-based spectrum disorder, although current studies indicate that genetics and environment both play a role. Even so, current research in cognitive science and neuroscience is teaching us more and more about how the brain works.

From this research, we are learning that the brain is a system of networks that are interconnected. These networks work in tandem, allowing us to process large amounts of simultaneous information usefully and effectively. To illustrate this idea, imagine you are sitting before a great symphony orchestra. With just the right timing, harmony, and loudness the conductor processes notes and instructions, which enables her to guide the many instruments, divided into five distinct groups, through a composition. Each member of the orchestra strives to play together as one, despite the fact that at times one hundred separate instruments make up the whole.

Our brain is that great symphony orchestra. The electroneural transmitters represent the notes, while different sections of our brain, referred to as *lobes*, represent the orchestra's instrument groups. The conductor, appropriately situated, represents the frontal lobe of our brain, the area I refer to as the *captain of the ship.* With the captain at the helm, the brain uniquely and amazingly blends a multitude of split-second messages, automatically, unleashing our human potential, the concert of all concerts. But what happens when the system fails? What happens when the uniquely human function of speech, language, and social communication fails? As I've discussed, we can describe what happens, but to date we do not know why.

For now, the diagnosis of a speech, language, and social disorder remains rudimentary, almost exclusively based on observation. The most overt characteristics are behavior outbursts, hypersensitivities, and at the core, speech-language delay. It is the speech-language delay that has been the essence of this book. As children reach eighteen months of age and are speaking with little to no words, resist social interaction, and at times appear deaf, it is of no surprise that parents are on high alert. Family, friends, and professionals, with good intentions, may try to minimize your concern by suggesting that you are overreacting. We have learned through many years of experience, however, that this is not the advice to take. If, in fact, you believe your child is delayed in language onset or at risk for ASD, research indicates the earlier the intervention, the better the outcome.

Unfortunately, even following your feelings does not mean that help is immediately on its way. Typically, children are not evaluated until eighteen to twenty-four months old. From the time of the evaluation until therapy begins, valuable time is being lost. Although the intervention process has begun, children often do not actually begin therapy until they near their third birthday. By this time, the many parents I have spoken with share a universal complaint, the feeling of *helplessness,* as more and more time is being wasted, without knowing what to do. That is why this book is so important. I don't want parents to feel helpless or frustrated any longer. I know there are ways you, as a parent, can begin to make a difference in your child's development. This book is all about empowering you, during a very stressful time in your life. It's all about letting you in on what I know and sharing it.

With a diagnosis of ASD, it is possible that your child may be facing life-long challenges. Learning words, playing appropriately, and understanding the world around him will take many trials, many times. Patience will be your most important ally, and I truly believe that with this book by your side you will be prepared to face the challenge. With an understanding of typical speech and language development, by making your home a language enriched experience, by knowing the right toys to buy, and by having strategies to stimulate your child's willingness and ability to communicate, you will become a proactive parent with a plan. In addition, by seeing examples of how language delayed children or at-risk children process, interpret, and misinterpret what they hear, the better able you will be to communicate more effectively with your own child. That's the goal of this book: to remove the helplessness by giving you guidance and tools. With this book you no longer need to sit back passively. You now have hands-on strategies, developmentally sound activities, and methods to record progress. You are now ready to be your child's *communication partner.* You are now able to be your child's educational advocate.

So here I will end. Theoretically, the development of this book began over twenty years ago, not in actual writing, but by recording the ways children communicate. By observing and documenting the words they used, messages they didn't understand, and questions they could not answer, I realized that I had accumulated a longitudinal wealth of valuable and useful information. I'm sharing this with you, but it's still not enough. Parents, teachers, and children need workbooks, coloring and vocabulary books presented with language-based goals. Parents need more education. Pediatricians need to include a developmental language screening as part of their protocol, along with weight, height, vision, and hearing. There is much more to do.

BIBLIOGRAPHY

Autism Society of America. "Facts and Statistics." Accessed December 28, 2010. http://www.autism-society.org/about-autism/facts-and-statistics.html.

AutismWeb. "A Parent's Guide to Autism Spectrum Disorders." Accessed December 28, 2010. http://www.autismweb.com/signs.htm.

Baron-Cohen, Simon. "Theory of Mind in Normal Development and Autism." *Prisme* 34 (2001): 174–83.

Bloom, Lois, and Margaret Lahey. *Language Development and Language Disorders.* Somerset, NJ: John Wiley & Sons, 1978.

Centers for Disease Control and Prevention. "Data & Statistics." Last modified May 13, 2010. Accessed December 28, 2010. http://www.cdc.gov/ncbddd/autism/data.html.

Grandin, Temple. *Thinking in Pictures: And Other Reports from My Life with Autism.* New York: Doubleday Dell Publishing Group, Inc., 1995.

Gullo, Dominic, and Jeanne Gullo. "An Ecological Language Intervention Approach with Mentally Retarded Adolescents." *Language, Speech, and Hearing Services in Schools* 15, no. 3 (1984): 182–91.

Marton, Klara. "Executive Function and Language Processing." Department of Speech Communication Arts & Sciences, Brooklyn College, CUNY, May 7, 2006.

Mauszycki, Shannon C., and Julie L. Wambaugh, "Acquired Apraxia of Speech: A Treatment Overview." *ASHA Leader*, April 26, 2011, 16–19.

Murray, Donna S., Lisa A. Ruble, Heather Willis, and Cynthia A. Molloy. "Parent and Teacher Report of Social Skills in Children with Autism Spectrum

Disorders." *Language, Speech, and Hearing Services in Schools* 40, no. 2 (2009): 109–15.

Pinker, Steven. *The Language Instinct: How the Mind Creates Language.* New York: William Morrow and Company, Inc., 1995.

Sander, E. "When Are Speech Sounds Learned?" *Journal of Speech and Hearing Disorders* 37 (1972): 62.

Watson, Linda R., and Michelle Flippin. "Language Outcomes for Young Children with Autism Spectrum Disorders." *ASHA Leader*, May 27, 2008, 8–12.

Wigg, Elisabeth, and Eleanor Semel. *Language Assessment and Intervention for the Learning Disabled*, 2nd ed. Columbus, OH: Charles E. Merrill Publishing Company, 1984.

Williams, D. L., G. Goldstein, and N. J. Minshew. "The Profile of Memory Function in Children with Autism." *Neuropsychology* 20, no. 1 (2006): 21–29. Accessed June 12, 2011. http://www.ncbi.nlm.nih.gov/pmc/articles/PMC1847594/?tool=pubmed.

Williams, Diane, and Nancy Minshew. "How the Brain Thinks in Autism: Implications for Language Intervention." *ASHA Leader*, April 27, 2010, 8–11.

LIST OF WEBSITES

We are lucky to be living at a time when information is just a click away. Although I have worked hard to offer you insight and understanding, in reality the amount of available material would fill volumes. As a result, I have selected a few websites you may like to visit. Each site provides you with additional information on speech and language development and delay. In addition, these sites introduce you to further sites where you can continue to expand your knowledge.

American Speech-Language-Hearing Association: http://www.asha.org/.
Babies and Sign Language: http://www.babies-and-sign-language.com/special-needs.html.
CafeMom: http://www.cafemom.com/profile/reg_landing.php?cb_id=autismsupport_ribbon_new&utm_medium=sem&utm_source=yahoo&utm_content=autism_group_newlp_mbus&utm_campaign=autism_newcamp_newlp&utm_term=autism%20resources&use_mobile=0&flow=autismsupport_group&SR=sr3_171701326_ms.
The Hanen Centre: http://www.hanen.org/Areas-of-Expertise/Early-Childhood-Language-Delays.aspx.
How to Teach a Child Sign Language: http://www.ehow.com/how_2077645_teach-child-sign-language.html.

KidsHealth.org: http://kidshealth.org/parent/emotions/behavior/not_
talk.html.

Learn ABA: http://www.learnaba.org/resources/.

Raising Children Network: http://raisingchildren.net.au/articles/
language_delay.html.

Sign Language for Kids: http://www.buzzle.com/articles/sign-language
-for-kids.html.

SpeechDelay.com: http://www.speechdelay.com/.

Teach Me to Talk: http://teachmetotalk.com/2008/07/15/discover
-the-best-approach-proven-to-teach-your-toddler-to-talk/?
gclid=CMOi4sb7-K8CFUQQNAod6jLeFA.

University of Michigan Health System, YourChild: www.med.umich
.edu/yourchild/topics/speech.htm.

INDEX

ABOUT THE AUTHOR

Barbara Levine Offenbacher is a New York State licensed speech language pathologist at the Manhattan Beach Speech Language Reading Center, where she maintains a full time private practice. She holds a certificate of clinical competence from the American Speech Language Hearing Association and is licensed by the state of New York as a teacher for the speech and hearing handicapped. After receiving her master's degree, she continued her education and received an advanced certificate in educational administration and supervision. Her career began as a speech language therapist in the New York City public school system. During those years she won numerous grants, but is most noted for winning the New York City Division of Curriculum and Instruction Impact II Grant, sponsored by the Exxon Corporation, where her program was awarded first place in the division of special education. She also served as an adjunct professor at the Brooklyn College Graduate School in the Department of Special Education. In gratitude for her professional success, Barbara founded the Kol Moshe Foundation, in memory of her parents. The mission of the foundation is to provide, clinical materials and money, as well as fostering better awareness of the challenges of communication disorders in both children and adults. The foundation has helped the communication impaired in both the United States and Israel. Barbara is married to Dr. Eliezer Offenbacher. They have two wonderful sons, a terrific daughter in law, and recently became grandparents for the first time. Currently they reside in the Manhattan Beach community in Brooklyn, New York.